D1263130

John Dalton

and the Development
of Atomic Theory

John Dalton
and the Development
of Atomic Theory

MORGAN
REYNOLDS
PUBLISHING

Greensboro, North Carolina

John Dalton and the Development of Atomic Theory

Library of Congress Cataloging-in-Publication Data

Baxter, Roberta, 1952-
John Dalton and the development of atomic theory / by Roberta Baxter.
    p. cm.
Includes bibliographical references.
ISBN 978-1-59935-122-3 ISBN 159935-122-6 (ebook)
1. Dalton, John, 1766-1844--Juvenile literature. 2. Chemists--Great
Britain--Biography--Juvenile literature. 3. Atomic theory--Juvenile
literature. I. Title.
QD22.D2B39 2011
509.2--dc22
[B]
                    2010038610

Printed in the United States of America
First Edition

Book Cover and interior designed by:
Ed Morgan, navyblue design studio
Greensboro, N.C.

Profiles in Science Series

John Dalton and the Development of Atomic Theory

Ernest Rutherford and the Birth of the Atomic Age

Nikola Tesla and the Taming of Electricity

Skeptical Chemist: The Story of Robert Boyle

New Elements: The Story of Marie Curie

Scheduling the Heavens: The Story of Edmond Halley

Rosalind Franklin and the Structure of Life

Ibn al-Haytham: First Scientist

Double Stars: The Story of Caroline Herschel

Illuminating Progress: The Story of Thomas Edison

Michael Faraday and the Nature of Electricity

Origin: The Story of Charles Darwin

Fire, Water, and Air: The Story of Antoine Lavoisier

The Great Explainer: The Story of Richard Feynman

John Dalton

Contents

1 A Quaker Boy   9

2 Young Teacher   17

3 Meteorological Observations and Essays   27

4 I'm Color-blind?   39

5 Fascination with Gases   49

6 The Atomic Theory Is Born   59

7 Controversy and New Symbols   71

8 Dalton Meets the King, and Other Honors   81

9 Legacy   91

Timeline   101
Sources   102
Bibliography   106
Web Sites   107
Index   108

Drawn & Etch'd by J. Stephenson

John Dalton,
D.C.L. L.L.D. F.R.S. L & E. &c &c

President of the
Lit: & Phil: Soc: Manch:

A Quaker Boy

John Dalton was famous in the scientific world, but when Monsieur Pelletan came from Paris, France, in 1820 to see the great man, he had trouble finding him. He thought he would find John in a distinguished position, surrounded by colleagues and students. Finally, he found him at the side of a boy and his slate. Monsieur Pelletan asked if he had the honor of addressing the famous Mr. Dalton. John replied, "Yes. Will you sit till I put this lad right about his arithmetic?"

This story, which may or may not be true, demonstrates that even though John Dalton was famous as founder of the Atomic Theory, he considered himself first a teacher. Outside of his teaching duties, he conducted experiments that clarified his ideas about the world around him. Through his writings and theories, he focused the eyes of the scientific community on topics such as the source of the aurora borealis, the cause of color-blindness, and the existence of the atom. His dual nature as scientist and teacher combined to form ideas that brought theoretical and practical chemistry into one compound.

His Quaker love of simplicity allowed him to cut away the conglomeration of wrong ideas and hone in on central truths about matter.

Many of Dalton's notebooks and original documents were stored at the institution where he worked for fifty years, the Manchester Literary and Philosophical Society in Manchester, England. Unfortunately, many of the items were destroyed in a fire after the German air force bombed Manchester on December 24, 1940. Less than a quarter of his documents were salvaged, and most of the remaining documents have charred edges and sections that were completely lost. So much of what we know about Dalton comes from early biographers, such as William Henry, Sir Henry Roscoe, and R. A. Smith.

John Dalton was born on either September 5 or 6, 1766. The exact date is not known because his birth, in an unusual occurrence, was not recorded in the records of the Quakers, a religious society. When he was older he talked to people in the village, and from their accounts he decided that he had been born on September 5.

John's grandfather, Jonathan, was a farmer and shoemaker who joined the Quakers. He married Abigail Fearon, also a Quaker, whose dowry included a small farm. Over time, Jonathan added sixty acres to the family holdings, which were inherited by their oldest son, also named Jonathan. Their second son, Joseph, lived in a small cottage on the family land. When Jonathan died without children, Joseph inherited the farm.

Joseph married Quaker Deborah Greenup, who was described as an "active-minded and energetic woman." Besides his brother Jonathan, Joseph had an older sister, Mary. Three other children did not survive into adulthood. The family lived in Eaglesfield, a tiny town in northwest England, in a small, thatched-roof cottage. Surrounding the town were beautiful fields, hills, and valleys. Joseph worked as a farmer and weaver in a time when the industry of weaving was still centered primarily in homes (called a cottage industry). Deborah contributed to the family income by selling inks and paper from their two-room home. The family often struggled to make ends meet.

The Daltons were members of the Religious Society of Friends, commonly known as the Quakers. George Fox had founded the group in England in 1652. In the years before John's birth, many more people had become Quakers. The Society protested the establishment of the Church of England as the official church, and so they were included in a group of churches called Dissenters.

Quakers believed strongly in the equality of all people. In fact, women were allowed to speak at their assemblies. All people were to be open to the calling of the Holy Spirit, a condition known as the "Inner Light," so anyone might be chosen to speak a message to the group. Meetings began in silence, which lasted until someone felt the need to speak.

They dressed plainly, usually in black and gray clothing, and sought simplicity in all areas of their lives. In speech, they used the words *thee* and *thou* instead of you when speaking to another. Because the names of the days of the week were derived from pagan gods, they instead called them "First Day," "Second Day," and so on. In the same way, months were also numbered.

Another characteristic of Society members was their strong emphasis on peace and social reform. Throughout history, Quakers often have been classified as conscientious objectors due to their refusal to bear arms in war. They also strongly opposed slavery in the United States, and many of the most active participants in the Underground Railroad were Quakers.

Because of his training as a Quaker, John Dalton always wore subdued clothing, and his speech included *thee* and *thou*. Being a Dissenter also prevented him from attending a national university, even if he had money to pay for it. Dalton didn't talk about his religious beliefs, even to friends or in letters, so we know little of his actual beliefs. However, all his life he attended weekly Quaker meetings and yearly conferences of the group.

An aspect of the Quakers that benefited John was their strong support of education. Not wanting their children to be contaminated by

A Quaker meeting in the seventeenth century

ways of the world, they established schools in which young ones could be trained in Quaker ideals. Students learned to read and write English, Latin (if a teacher was available for the subject), public speaking, arithmetic, and even some upper mathematics. The Bible was used as a primary text. Since only one in 215 people in England could read at the time, attending school was a privilege.

Those of Dissenter religions often established schools called Dissenting Academies, which were well known. They were called "the greatest schools of their day. During a period when the grammar schools slept and when the universities were sterile, the Dissenting Academies were not merely in existence, but were thoroughly alive and active, doing remarkably good work."

One advantage of the schools was an emphasis on hands-on learning in nature and crafts. By understanding nature, Quakers believed that they better understood God, the creator.

John attended the local Quaker school at Pardshaw Hall, about two miles from the village of Eaglesfield. His teacher, John Fletcher, was thoroughly devoted to teaching. John showed no exceptional ability in his studies, but he was noted for his tenacity. According to one story, he struggled to find a solution to a mathematics problem. When questioned about the answer, he said in his thick dialect, "Yan med due't." (One might do it.) After more time and still no answer, he said, "I can't deu't to-neet, but mebby tomorn I will." (I can't do it tonight, but maybe tomorrow I will.) According to biographer Henry Roscoe, Dalton did have the answer the next morning. Many creative people find that sleeping on a problem brings an answer.

In one account, discussion broke among workers in a field about whether sixty yards square and sixty square yards are the same area. John at first believed they were the same, but after consideration of the problem, he realized that they were not equal.

John's abilities caught the attention of Elihu Robinson, a well-to-do Quaker living in Eaglesfield. Robinson, Fletcher, and others formed a reading club and brought books and magazines from London for their enjoyment. Robinson also corresponded with scientists from around the world, including Benjamin Franklin.

Robinson tutored John and another young man, William Alderson, in mathematics. Robinson was also an amateur meteorologist and took daily weather readings. Before long, John also adopted this practice.

When John was twelve, Fletcher left the school. No one else was hired as teacher, so John began his own school. It was time for him to contribute to the family income, so he printed up signs for lessons "for both sexes at reasonable terms."

From all accounts, John's introduction to teaching was rocky. The school was held in a barn, then in the Dalton cottage, and finally in

Isaac Newton's handwritten solution of the brachystochrone, or curve of quickest descent. Dalton would be heavily influenced by Newton.

the local Quaker meeting house. Students ranged from those just learning their letters to boys older than John. In later years, one of his students remembered that boys often challenged John to fight. One time, he locked some students in the school to force them to finish their work; they broke windows and escaped. Still, the townspeople did not hold a grudge against John for the discipline problems.

Visits to his friend Elihu Robinson stimulated John's mind. He copied the entire text of a magazine that he probably borrowed from Robinson. It was called *The Ladies' Diary, or Woman's Almanac of 1779*, which claimed to boast "new improvements in arts and sciences and many entertaining particulars, designed for the use and diversion of the fair sex." *The Ladies' Diary* provided poetry, puzzles, and literature of interest to men and women. A newer counterpart, *The Gentleman's Diary, or the Mathematical Repository*, contained "many useful and entertaining particulars adapted to the ingenious gentlemen engaged in the delightful study and practice of mathematics." It also provided mathematical and logic problems. Famous mathematicians and scientists from around England contributed puzzles, enigmas, and scientific facts for the readers to solve and enjoy. Readers were encouraged to submit solutions.

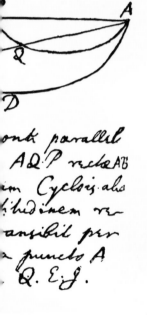

John's name appears in a 1787 edition of *The Ladies' Diary*, as he submitted the answer to an algebra problem. Prizes were given for the most correct answers, and that year John answered thirteen of fifteen problems to finish in first place. In 1789, he received a prize of six issues of *The Ladies' Diary*. He also won first place in a contest for *The Gentleman's Diary* by solving a difficult hydrostatics problem.

Over the next twenty years, his name appeared often in the pages of both magazines, with solutions to math problems, comments on natural science, and even short takes on topics such as "Friendship and Love" and "Divorce." These essays must have been based on the relationships he knew about, because as far as we know, John never seriously considered marriage.

John's teaching pay was not enough to support him. After two years, he gave up the school and worked as a farmer for about a year. He might have remained a farmer, but he was ambitious to do other things.

The area where John lived is called the Lake District. It is a beautiful region of hills, valleys, lakes, and streams. A group of poets who lived there in the early 1800s became known as the Lake Poets. William Wordsworth wrote a poem entitled "Daffodils" that describes the bright flowers dancing at a lake's edge. The other Lake Poets were Samuel Taylor Coleridge and Robert Southey. As part of the Romantic literature movement, they immortalized the region in their poems.

Just as the poets were influenced by the beauty of the Lake District, Dalton was inspired by the area's landscape to study weather and gases. He soon moved to another section of the region. In 1781, John left Eaglesfield for Kendal, about forty-five miles away. But during the summers for the rest of his life, he would return to the Lake District. One of his favorite excursions was scaling Helvellyn, a mountain that rose to 3,100 feet.

Young Teacher

At age twelve, John Dalton became the teacher at the school where he had been a student. For most of the rest of his life, he was teaching in one form or another. Teaching did not pay well, so for a short time during his adolescence, he farmed some land for his uncle.

In 1781, he returned to teaching. His brother Jonathan had been teaching at a Quaker school in Kendal that was owned by a cousin, George Bewley. Jonathan asked John to join him as a teacher at the school.

On the forty-five mile journey from Eaglesfield, John traveled through Cockermouth, where he spotted the finest in accessories for the young gentleman—an umbrella. John had not seen an umbrella before, but since he believed he was moving up in the world, he bought one.

After the Dalton sons had taught at the school for about four years, Bewley decided to retire. Jonathan and John apparently persuaded their father to take out a mortgage on the farm to help them buy the school. Their sister Mary came to Kendal to keep house for the brothers and the boarders at the school.

An advertisement for the school stated that "Jonathan & John Dalton respectfully inform their Friends and the Public in General, that they intend to continue the school taught by George Bewley, where Youth will be carefully instructed in English, Latin, Greek & French; also writing, arithmetic, merchants' accounts, and the mathematics."

Over the following year, the brothers added the subjects of surveying, algebra, optics, mechanics, and other technical topics to the curriculum. The teaching pay still was meager, so John also gave private tutoring lessons and lectures. He was twenty-one years old and had not started scientific experiments, but he studied what science books he could obtain and made his own observations. He arranged a set of "Twelve lectures of Natural Philosophy [science] to be read at the school (if a sufficient number of subscribers are procured) by John Dalton." The cost of the lectures was half a guinea for the whole set or a shilling for a single lecture. Topics included mechanics—laws of motion, vibration of pendulums; optics—doctrine of colors, spectacles, telescopes, microscopes, and the rainbow; pneumatics—the elasticity of air, description of the air pump; and many other scientific subjects.

Some of their students later described the brothers as harsh teachers, though John was milder than his brother. The usual punishment for a serious offense in a Quaker school was beating, and it seems that the brothers followed this rule. Students remembered that John often became absorbed in mathematical problems, scribbling them on scraps of paper that ended up everywhere. Students often took advantage of his distracted state to do what they wanted.

Unfortunately, a diary that John kept through the years was lost, so we depend on the memories of his friends to learn about him. In spite of his stern behavior as a teacher, he was a cheerful, easygoing young man. He kept careful records of expenses and income and of occurrences in his life. One friend, Peter Clare, remembered that at one party, the people entertained themselves by making up verses. Each person would add a few lines, and the next person had to compose lines that rhymed with the previous lines. John wrote the entire set of verses down when he got home, along with the name of the person who composed each set.

While in Kendal, John met a man who would influence his life and be his lifelong friend. John Gough, who belonged to one of the wealthiest families in town, had been blinded by a case of smallpox when he was a toddler. He also had epilepsy. Refusing to let his health problems prevent him from learning, he trained himself to solve math problems in his head and learned languages, physics, botany, and zoology. Famous poet William Wordsworth wrote of him in a poem called *The Excursion*:

> Methinks I see him now, his eyeballs roll'd
> Beneath his ample brow—in darkness pained,
> But each instinct with spirit, and the freame
> Of the whole countenance alive with thought,
> Fancy, and understanding, whilst the voice
> Discoursed of natural or moral truth
> With eloquence and such authentic power,
> That in his presence humbler knowledge stood
> Abashed, and tender pity overawed.

In a letter to his friend Peter Crosthwaite, written in 1788, Dalton wrote that by smell, feel, and taste Gough could identify nearly every plant for twenty miles around. He added, "He is, perhaps, one of the most astonishing instances that ever appeared of what genius, united with perseverance and every other subsidiary aid, can accomplish when deprived of what we usually reckon the most valuable sense." Dalton often served as Gough's secretary to record observations and mathematical solutions. In a book written by Dalton years later, he wrote, "Mr. Gough was as much gratified with imparting his stores of science as I was in receiving them."

Dalton's friends Elihu Robinson, in Eaglesfield, and Peter Crosthwaite, in Keswick, made and recorded meteorological observations.

Gough, who was also an amateur meteorologist, encouraged Dalton to begin his own studies. On March 24, 1787, Dalton began a meteorological journal, a practice he continued for the rest of his life. The first notation in his journal says, "In the evening, soon after sunset, there appeared a remarkable aurora borealis, the sky being generally clear and the moon shining; it spread over above one-half of the hemisphere, appeared very vivid, and had a quick vibratory motion; about eight the heavens were overcast, and the aurora almost disappeared." Dalton's study of weather and the atmosphere would lead to his greatest ideas.

Instruments available to the amateur meteorologist at the time were expensive, so Dalton usually constructed his own. Thermometers, barometers, hygrometers (which measure humidity), and wind and rain gauges served as his instruments. He even sold some of the thermometers and barometers that he had made. When he could afford it, he invested in better instruments.

Dalton's journals of observations contain listings of his instruments in a format that resembles a spreadsheet. The area was one of mountains, valleys, and lakes, so the weather was frequently changing and often violent. Dalton's observations provide a record of the weather wherever he lived.

While in Kendal, Dalton also studied botany. Since he was always looking for a way to earn more money, he collected botanical specimens from the area and offered them to his friend Crosthwaite, who had started a small museum. Dalton wrote: "[I] dried and pressed a good many plants, and pasted them down to sheets of white paper, and found that they look very pretty, and attract the attention of all, both learned and unlearned; this has induced me to think that a tolerable collection of them, treated in this manner, would be a very proper object in the museum. I cannot say what kind of recompense would be equivalent to such a task, but think I could engage to fill a book of two quires for half-a-guinea."

Dalton completed the book and, in October 1791, sold it to Crosthwaite's museum. He labeled the plants with both English and Linnean names. He also collected butterflies and other insects for the museum, observed the metamorphosis of caterpillars, and experimented on mites, maggots, and snails. He felt that "nothing that enjoys animal life, or that vegetates, is beneath the dignity of a naturalist to examine."

The town of Kendal, where John was teaching, was fairly large for the time—approximately 5,000 people. The more urban town provided magazines of popular culture, including *The Ladies' Diary* and *The Gentleman's Diary*, both of which continued to publish contributions from Dalton. Some of his mathematical solutions won prizes, which were generally free copies of the magazine.

In 1787, Joseph Dalton died. He thought that the family farm was entailed, meaning the law required it to be inherited only by the oldest son. Actually it wasn't, but John probably would not have desired to farm it anyway. Jonathan took over the farm, and John remained as a teacher in Kendal. Still, the low pay and constant struggle of teaching discouraged him. He began to think about other professions and asked advice from his friends about the possibilities.

Dalton pressed native flowers and plants to
create his botanical book of plants.

In a letter to Elihu Robinson, he wrote, "The occasion of my addressing thee at this time is a projected change of my occupation, which I have been meditating on for some time past." He went on to explain that teaching pay was so low that few made a decent living and that he had been considering different professions. He wrote, "At the head of these stand law and physic [medicine]. Whether of these professions would be more likely for me to make a livelihood, or whether would require more time or expense to attain, I cannot tell; but, interest being set aside, I should much prefer the latter."

Next, he listed his estimation of the cost of studying medicine in Edinburgh, Scotland. He asked Robinson's opinion on his idea, and then—as if he was studying medicine already—he listed some experiments with digestion. He had measured and recorded in his notebook everything he ate, as well as "Evacuation S[olid?] L[iquid?] Perspiration, etc." He copied his results in the letter.

Robinson's response to Dalton's projected career change was negative. "As I have thought thy talents were well adapted to thy present profession, I cannot say thy proposal of changing it was very welcome to me, believing thou wouldst not only shine but be really useful in that noble labour of teaching youth."

Dalton also wrote to his uncle, Thomas Greenup, who practiced the profession of law. The answer: "I think they are both [law and medicine] totally out of the reach of a person in thy circumstances."

In a letter to his cousin, George Bewley, Dalton acknowledged that Bewley and Greenup agreed that he should not change careers. He added that "I cannot say that I have yet fully determined respecting myself." The rest of the letter was about scientific books that he had read, especially with an eye toward medicine, and their value. He also wished to know of more good books on topics such as anatomy and chemistry.

In 1793, on the recommendation of John Gough, John received an appointment as professor in mathematics and natural philosophy at New College in Manchester. His pay for teaching from September to June would be eighty pounds. Living arrangements required him to

The Town Hall clock tower in Manchester, England

pay the college twenty-seven pounds and ten shillings, so the pay was not high. However, it was more than he had made in Kendal.

So John moved to Manchester, the city in which he would spend the rest of his life. He never married, but there are indications that he fell in love a couple times. When asked in later life why he had never married, he would reply that he never had time.

In 1795, Dalton met the son and two daughters of the Jepson family. Over a year's time, he visited them several times. He and the son became good friends, once taking a walking tour together. Dalton seemed particularly drawn to the older daughter, Hannah. In a letter to his brother, Dalton wrote that people might wonder if he would ever marry, but he added, "I may answer that my head is too full of triangles, chymical processes, and electrical experiments, etc. to think of marriage." But then he went on to admit that he had recently admired a woman, one with "the most perfect figure that human eyes ever beheld, in a plain but neat dress." Her conversation about literary topics, grammar, and scientific ideas captivated Dalton. "During my *captivity*, which lasted about a week, I lost my appetite, and had other symptoms of *bondage* about me, as incoherent discourse, etc., but have now happily regained my freedom."

In a later letter, he praised both sisters, but cautioned his brother that he would not want anyone to know his feelings. He visited Hannah after her brother's death in 1797, but nothing came of the relationship. In 1801, she married and moved to Bristol. Forty years later, Dalton was able to visit her and her family during a scientific conference.

Dalton's early biographer, Henry Roscoe, said that in the collection of Dalton's belongings at the Manchester Literary and Philosophical Society, he found "a dried specimen of the lady's slipper . . . a charming orchid, very abundant in the Yorkshire dales in 1790, but now scarce even in its most favourite haunts. Under this specimen, I found in Dalton's handwriting the following inscription: 'Presented to me by Nancy Wilson, of Thornton-in-Craven.'"

A friend of Dalton's in later life, Miss Johns, said that he had mentioned a Quaker friend who had died young, and he would say, with tears, "Poor Nancy, poor Nancy."

While still at Kendal, Dalton had collected months of weather observations. By the time he moved to Manchester, the book he had written about meteorology was ready for print.

Meteorological Observations and Essays

With his hopes of a profession in law or medicine quashed, John Dalton turned to what he knew. His friends had piqued his interest in meteorology—the study of weather. He kept meticulous, daily records and corresponded with others, such as Peter Crosthwaite, who also recorded readings. The area around Eaglesfield and Kendal provided a conglomeration of weather to observe. The landscape of hills, lakes, and valleys caused variations in weather, sometimes in just a few hours.

Dalton began writing a series of lectures and essays that would become his first published work: *Meteorological Observations and Essays*. The book was published after he moved to Manchester in 1793, but the work had been written while he was teaching in Kendal.

It is obvious that the book was written by a teacher. Part I covers making instruments, including a thermometer, barometer, hygrometer, and rain gauge. He wrote: "As the number of these is increasing daily, many of them must fall into hands that are much unacquainted with their principles, and may therefore not profit by them in so great a degree as others; for which reason a short and clear explanation with a series of observations serving further to illustrate and exemplify the Principles and a few Practical rules for judging of the weather . . . would be an addition to the stock already before the public, and might perhaps be found subservient to the improvement of the science."

The first part of the manuscript is the Observations portion. Part I, Section 1 begins with instructions for making a barometer, including how to ensure that the mercury is dry. He covered the idea that air has weight because the atmosphere extends from "supposed 40 to 50 miles." Proof of that weight had been shown by placing barometers in the chambers of air pumps. He credited Italian scientist Torricelli with the invention of the barometer and stated that "[the] discovery promised to be of utmost importance to mankind, by enabling them to foresee those changes in the atmosphere." But he added that the promise of the barometer had not been completely fulfilled. The fact is that many conditions besides the barometric reading affect the weather,

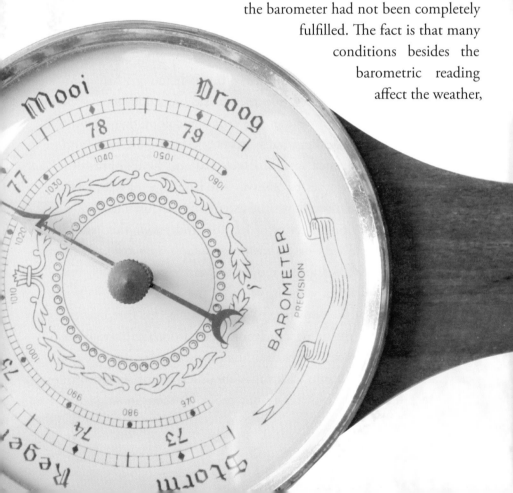

and even today meteorologists still can miss a forecast because of the huge amounts of data that affect weather.

As examples, Dalton added charts of barometric readings that he had taken in Kendal and Crosthwaite had recorded in Keswick twenty-two miles away. He also included readings taken in London by members of the Royal Society that were published in their magazine. Kendal's and Keswick's measurements were taken three times a day: morning, noon, and evening. His charts give the mean, the high, and the low of barometer readings for Kendal and Keswick.

In the next section, Dalton wrote about the thermometer. He noted that the thermometer was invented before the barometer but not perfected until later. Until mercury or other liquids were enclosed in evacuated tubes, the thermometer had been affected by air pressure just as a barometer was, rising or falling with the air pressure plus the temperature. Once thermometers were improved, only the temperature would register on the thermometer.

In this section, Dalton dived into a discussion of heat that was raging at the time. What is heat and cold? How is it measured? What is its source? He wrote: "Philosophers [scientists] are generally persuaded, that the sensations of heat and cold are occasioned by the presence or absence, in degree, of a certain principle or quality denominated *fire* or *heat*:—thus when any substance feels cold, it is concluded the principle of heat is not so abundant in that substance as in the hand; and if it feels hot, it is more abundant. It is more probable, that all substances whatever contain more or less of this principle."

Dalton stated that scientists had not agreed on what heat was. Scientists disagreed about whether heat was a quality, or a substance, or a property of matter. Some scientists, such as Isaac Newton, believed it arises from "an internal vibratory motion of the particles of bodies." Dalton didn't specify here which notion he accepted. However, he went on to describe that matter, especially gases, expand due to increased heat, and he applied that concept to the construction of a thermometer. He explained standardizing the degrees marked on thermometers with the boiling and freezing points of water. Scientists used thermometers with differing amounts of degrees between boiling and freezing points of water. Reaumer's scale, for example, marked off 80 degrees between the boiling and freezing points of water. Others used the Fahrenheit scale, with freezing water at 32 degrees and boiling at 212. Dalton felt that all should use the same scale.

While showing the tables of temperature records, Dalton noted that the temperatures at Keswick often read high. He theorized that the sun shone on the thermometer for some portion of the day, and it also received reflected heat from the ground. His thoughtful consideration of these conditions demonstrated his careful methods. As with the barometer, he gave mean, high, and low readings.

In Section 3, Dalton explained the construction and use of a hygrometer, "an instrument meant to show the disposition of the air for attracting water, or for depositing the water it has in solution with it." In other words, it measures humidity. He described his hygrometer as a length of whipcord fastened with a nail at one end and looped over a pulley with weights that stretched the other end out. Measurements in tenths of an inch were taken to see how long the cord was stretched. He wrote, "the greater the number of the scale, the longer is the string, and the drier the air." He realized that the mean length of string was increasing each year, and he concluded that adjustments had to be made to compare the measurements from year to year. He also stated that his instrument showed a variation in the dryness or dampness of the air, but "it is very inadequate to the purpose for which a hygrometer is desired."

Rain gauges are discussed in the next section, including rainfall measurements at Kendal and Keswick. He included the highest amount at Kendal as 4.592 inches on April 22, 1792.

The next section is entitled "Observations on the heights of Clouds." Crosthwaite had used nearby mountains and a telescope to determine the heights of clouds over a five-year time span. Measurements could be taken only on partly cloudy days and when the cloud tops were below the mountaintop. Dalton made only one statement about these measurements—that the idea that cloud heights rise and fall with barometric readings is not true.

The next three sections list the occurrence of thunderstorms and hail, high winds, and the first frost and snow. Section 9 recounts a listing of high winds and waves on a lake near Keswick based on measurements of Crosthwaite. The observations of Dalton and Crosthwaite provide an excellent record of weather for this area of England.

Section 10 includes a list of sightings of the aurora borealis, or the northern lights. Wrote Dalton, "Sometimes the appearance is that of a large, still, luminous arch, or zone, resting upon the northern horizon, with a fog at the bottom; at other times, flashes or coruscations, are seen over a great part of the hemisphere." He described the brilliance, colors, and activity level of each aurora noted.

In Section 11, Dalton gave a lecture on magnetism, stating that understanding of the phenomenon is essential to understanding the other sections on the aurora and an essay about the northern lights. As a true teacher, he covered lodestones, compass needles, magnetic poles, attraction, and repulsion.

In an addendum to the book, Dalton included more observations and conjectures about the aurora. He stated that many had tried to determine the height of the aurora, with suggestions ranging from a thousand feet to a thousand miles. He reported that the aurora must be a considerable height because there were records of auroras at the same times in many different places in northern England. Dalton had a new instrument, called a theodolite, which measured vertical angles, and he used it to calculate the height. By collecting altitude measurements from places in England and Scotland, Dalton deduced that the distance was great enough to provide an accurate measurement. Because the two points were miles apart and both measured about the same altitude for the aurora, he knew that the height measurement was accurate. The measurement showed that the curve of the arch followed the curve of the earth. He wrote, "The height of the arch was found one hundred miles or upwards." Now we know that the atmosphere affected by the auroras reaches about two hundred miles.

The aurora borealis swirling over
Fairbanks, Alaska, the auroral capital of the world.

In the essay about the auroras, Dalton wrote that many people had observed that a compass needle was deflected during an aurora. He also had observed that the arch of an aurora is bisected by the magnetic meridian. He included geometric drawings that illustrated the planes of the aurora in relation to the Earth. So he concluded that "the beams were guided, not by gravity, but by the earth's magnetism."

In writing about the light of the aurora, Dalton stated, "The light of the aurora has been accounted for on three or more suppositions: 1. It has been supposed to be a flame arising from a chymical [chemical] effervescence of combustible exhalations from the earth. 2. It has been supposed to be inflammable air, fired by electricity. 3. It has been supposed electric light itself."

He demolished the first supposition because it did not account for all the characteristics of the aurora. He eliminated the second because it had been shown that the atmosphere is a mixture of gases, which doesn't allow the formation of strata of gas that would combust and cause the light. He demonstrated that the third was possible because lightning takes place in the atmosphere. He speculated that the light of the aurora comes not from combustion of a material in the atmosphere, but from a type of electric light similar to the discharge seen in the vacuum at the top of a barometer. In his opinion, the upper atmosphere might contain a gas that has magnetic properties.

Today we know that the auroras, both aurora borealis in the northern hemisphere and the aurora australis in the southern, form from charged electrons streaming in solar wind that interact with oxygen and nitrogen atoms in the atmosphere. Solar winds blast away from the sun at speeds of a million miles an hour and funnel along the Earth's magnetic lines of force. The colors of the aurora are determined by which atoms are struck in the atmosphere and by the altitude the collision occurs. For example, green comes from oxygen atoms hit at an altitude of up to 150 miles. Purple tints appear when nitrogen above sixty miles is struck, and blue shows up when the nitrogen is below sixty miles.

Dalton's work on the aurora was not groundbreaking, as many others were performing similar work. However, his conclusions were ahead of his time. At a time when electrons were unknown and magnetic force was just beginning to be comprehended, he put his observations together into a theory of the aurora's link to the magnetic field of the Earth.

In the first essay in *Meteorological Observations and Essays*, Dalton wrote about the atmosphere. He stated that the atmosphere is a mixture of gases and that the contour of the atmosphere must be the same as the Earth's because of gravity. For estimates of the height of the atmosphere, he declared that the most accurate measurement comes from barometric readings at different heights.

In other essays, Dalton proposed ideas about how wind occurs (by the sun heating the air, plus the rotation of the Earth), why barometer readings vary (connected to the moisture level of the air, according to Dalton), the relation between heat and other bodies, and the temperatures of different climates and seasons. His explanation for wind had already been proposed by other scientists, but his isolation and lack of resources, such as scientific journals, kept him from knowing the works of others.

In an essay entitled "On Evaporation: Rain, Hail, Snow and Dew," we get a glimpse of the importance of water vapor to Dalton.

His contemplation of the phenomenon of water in air would lead to his greatest discoveries.

In the first paragraphs, he refused to choose between two theories about evaporation: Is the water chemically combined with the other gases of the air, or is it diffused among them? But later, he disagreed with the chemical explanation by pointing out that evaporation occurs more rapidly when heat is applied, when the air is dry, and under decreased pressure. He provided a chart of experiments showing that the boiling point of water decreases as pressure decreases. "Upon consideration of the facts, it appears to me, that evaporation and the condensation of vapour are not the effects of chemical affinities, but that aqueous vapour always exists as a fluid sui generis [a class alone], diffused amongst the rest of the aerial fluids." In other words, water vapor exists as a gas along with the other gases of the atmosphere.

In a section explaining rain, hail, and snow, Dalton mentioned an abstract of an article in a scientific magazine. That article hypothesized that rain precipitates out of the air like a solid precipitating out of a supersaturated solution. Dalton theorized that rain comes from vapor being "condensed into water by cold." He explained the formation of dew by the fact that the surface of the Earth is colder at night than the air above it, leading to condensation of water vapor. In modern meteorological terms, this is referred to as the dew point and is a measure of the relative humidity of the air. When the humidity is high, the dew point is close to the actual temperature at the time.

In his seventh essay, Dalton began, "Since the barometer has become an instrument of general use, and is adopted as a guide by most people interested in the state of the weather, it may be of service to investigate the relation subsisting betwixt the weight of atmosphere and its disposition for rain, from the facts afforded us by observation." He proceeded to show that in months of low mean barometric readings, more rain fell. Dalton was not the first to observe this relation. Robert Boyle, 130 years earlier, had predicted a severe storm when the barometer fell to the lowest level he had seen. He was right—a storm of historic measure hit England. Other scientists had followed barometric readings and come to the same conclusion as Dalton, but his charts vividly display the connection.

In the second edition of his book, Dalton gave an explanation for the duration of some thunder. He mentioned a peal that he had heard that seemed to go on and on, and he stated that he doubted if the sound could be simply the result of the thunder echoing. He wrote, "a thought occurred to me, that if we could admit of an electric discharge to be made *instantly* from one cloud to another, through an extensive range of atmosphere, say twelve or fourteen miles, rather than from one cloud to another in the immediate vicinity, as within a few hundred feet or yards, we might give a much better explanation, both of the continuance and the irregularity of the sound." Even in a thunderstorm, Dalton was considering what caused the events around him.

Dalton's study of the weather led him to consider the atmosphere, gases, and their reactions with one another. *Meteorological Observations and Essays* would be reprinted in 1834, forty years later.

By moving to Manchester in 1793, Dalton had entered a larger scientific arena, one that would enrich his life. His experiments and conclusions led him to his greatest theory. But he also had a personal interest in something else—the study of vision.

I'm Color-blind?

In Manchester, Dalton taught at New College, a Dissident institution established to provide an education to those not allowed to attend national universities. It was started by Unitarian members, but it accepted students and teachers from other religions. Three courses of study were available: one for ministers, one for "other learned professions," and one for men planning commercial or government work. Each student was required to study mathematics and science.

The head of the school, Dr. Thomas Barnes, had written to John Gough requesting referrals of "a gentleman to fill the situation of Professor of Mathematics and Natural Philosophy in the new college, Mosley street, Manchester." Gough recommended Dalton. The position offered Dalton three guineas per student, with a total not less than eighty guineas. He was required to teach twenty-one hours a week in mathematics, mechanics, geometry, algebra, bookkeeping, natural philosophy, and chemistry.

Chetham's Library was founded in 1653 and is the oldest public library in the English-speaking world.

"Our academy is a large and elegant building in the most elegant and retired street of the place," Dalton wrote to his brother. He added details about the school and the town. "There is in this town a large library, furnished with the best books in every art, science and language, which is open to all gratis [free]." Chetham's Library contained almost 7,000 books and proved to be an important, critical boost to the availability of scientific knowledge to Dalton.

Dalton was also able to attend scientific lectures. A series by Thomas Garnett may have sparked his interest in chemistry. Although Dalton was teaching the subject based on his reading and own experiments, this was probably his first exposure to a teacher of chemistry. Garnett gave twelve lectures on natural philosophy [science] and thirty on chemistry. The topics included chemical techniques applied to practical applications, such as in agriculture, dyeing, and bleaching.

In Manchester, Dalton became acquainted with an interesting family. Thomas Henry had moved there in 1764 and began experimenting with magnesia alba. He developed a magnesia product and became rich selling it. He was known as Magnesia Henry. Thomas's youngest son, William, started at medical school and then returned to Manchester to help run the family business. In his spare time, while performing chemistry experiments, he discovered an important law, known as Henry's Law. William's son, William Charles Henry, became Dalton's first biographer.

Another crucial group in his development was the Manchester Literary and Philosophical Society, usually called the Lit & Phil. Founded by twenty-four leading citizens, the Lit & Phil provided a forum for discussion of scientific matters, as well as other topics. The rules listed the following as appropriate discussion topics: "natural philosophy, theoretical and experimental chemistry, polite literature, civil law, general politics, commerce and the arts."

Dalton was elected to the group in 1794. He remained a member and officer for the rest of his life. Members of the club included sixty ordinary members and several honorary ones from other places, including Joseph Priestley, Antoine Lavoisier, Alexander Volta, and Benjamin Franklin.

Dalton attended his first meeting on October 3. By the next meeting, he had a presentation to make to the group.

On October 31, 1794, Dalton read a paper before the Lit & Phil. It was entitled "Extraordinary facts relating to the Vision of Colours with Observations." He had investigated the phenomenon after discovering that he did not see as other people did.

According to one story, he gave his mother a pair of red stockings for her birthday. The store had advertised them as "Silk, and newest fashion," so they would be a welcome gift to his mother, who usually wore rough, thick stockings that she had knitted herself. When she received them, she told John, "Thou has bought me a grand pair of hose, John, but what made thee fancy such a bright colour? Why I can never show myself at meeting [Quaker church service] in them." When John replied that he thought they were blue, his mother answered, "Why, they're as red as a cherry, John." His brother also saw that blue color. The story may or may not be true, but we do have Dalton's description of his vision in his paper.

During the time he was working on botany—classifying plants, drying them, and plating them for the Keswick museum—he had trouble with colors. "Since the year 1790, the occasional study of botany obliged me to attend more to colours than before," he wrote. "With respect to colours that were *white, yellow,* or *green,* I readily assented to the appropriate term. *Blue, purple, pink* and *crimson* appeared rather less distinguishable; being, according to my idea, all referable to *blue.* I have often seriously asked a person whether a flower was blue or pink, but was generally considered to be in jest."

Dalton was near-sighted, requiring glasses to see far-away objects. However, his nearsightedness did not account for his inability to clearly distinguish colors. Dalton had what today is called color-blindness or color deficiency.

During his investigations, he also discovered that the color of a flower appeared different to him depending on the source of the light—sun or candle. He wrote, "Notwithstanding this, I was never convinced of a peculiarity in my vision, till I accidentally observed the colour of the flower of the Geranium zonale by candle-light, in the Autumn of 1792. The flower was pink, but it appeared to me almost an exact sky-blue by day; in candle-light, however, it was astonishingly changed, not having then any blue in it, but being what I called red, a colour which forms a striking contrast to blue."

When he asked others about the difference in the flower's color, he found that they saw it as pink in both daylight and candlelight. However, his brother Jonathan saw the same change in apparent color that John did. He continued, "This observation clearly proved, that my vision was not like that of other persons."

A prism splits white light into the full spectrum.

Dalton's scientific curiosity was aroused, and he began a study of his vision and that of others. Using a prism to break sunlight into a spectrum, he determined that most people could "distinguish six kinds of colour in the solar image: namely, *red, orange, yellow, green, blue,* and *purple.* To me it is quite otherwise—I see only *two* or at most

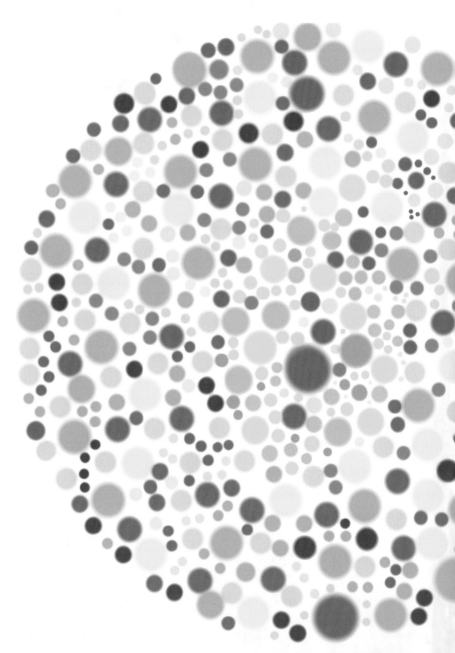

A color-blind test showing the number six

three, distinctions. These I should call yellow and blue; or yellow, blue, and purple. My yellow comprehends the *red, orange yellow,* and *green* of others; and my *blue* and *purple* coincide with theirs." In the paper, he contended, "Woollen yarn dyed crimson or dark blue is the same to me."

After determining that Jonathan's vision was the same as his, John began to test other people. He used a set of colored ribbons as the test material, along with questions on the perceptions of such things as grass, blood, the sky, etc. When he learned of an article about a family that also had color vision problems, he wrote a friend who lived in their city to see if they would be tested. His friend complied and sent a detailed report back to Dalton, showing that the family had four brothers out of six who did not see colors in the normal way. Dalton also tested his friends, his family members, and his students at New College until he had a group of about twenty people who had color vision deficiencies.

He found that these people all had problems with the red end of the light spectrum. To Dalton, a leaf and a stick of red sealing wax appeared the same. To him, the color of blood looked like the color called bottle green. "Hence it will be immediately concluded that I see either red or green, or both, different from other people. The fact is, I believe that they both appear different to me from what they do to others."

Another characteristic of this type of color deficiency was the difference in vision during daylight and candlelight. He wrote, "the difference between

day-light and candlelight, on some colours was indefinitely more per-
ceptible to me than to others."

Dalton also reported that all of the people with deficient vision
were males and that many from the same family might be affected. The
parents or children of the color deficient men had normal vision.

The condition that Dalton described came to be known as Daltonism in continental Europe.

In his biography of Dalton, published in 1895, Sir Henry Roscoe
noted that the type of vision that Dalton had could be dangerous for
people steering ships or driving trains. Many tests were being used to
identify the problem; some were accurate and others were not. Therefore, in the middle of the nineteenth century, the Royal Society had
been asked to determine the best method for testing for color deficiency.
In a demonstration of the test given by an official of one of the English
railroad companies, the assistant secretary of the Royal Society, Mr. Rix,
was tested and passed. When the tester was informed that Mr. Rix was
in fact color-blind, he said, "I must admit that Mr. Rix being colour-
blind is an eye opener!" Obviously, a better test for color-blindness
was needed so that the public could be sure that train engineers could
distinguish between a red danger light and a green safe one.

Today we understand much more about the structure of the eye.
Two types of cells, rods and cones, are present in the retina. The cones
contain three types of pigments that allow us to see colors: red, blue,
and green light. For example, the cones that are responsive to light in
wavelengths of 420 allow us to see blue to violet colors. Those sensitive
to wavelengths of 535 show up as the color green. The combination of
the response of the cones to the various wavelengths allows us to see all
the colors of the spectrum. A person with normal vision distinguishes
colors with wavelengths from 450 to 650 nm (nanometers; a nanome-
ter is one-billionth of a meter). For a person with color-blindness, the
visual spectrum is shifted. Dalton's vision was that of a protanope, one
who has low sensitivity to light in the red wavelengths.

Dalton concluded that his vision problems were due to a blue
coloring in the vitreous humour of the eye. He appears to have been

unaware of the fact that a bluish tint in that part of his eye would have no effect on red, yellow, orange, or green color distinction. In his will, he asked that his eyes be examined after death to determine if this was true. A contemporary of Dalton's, Thomas Young, suggested in 1802 that the retina might contain three vibrating systems that allowed humans to see color. He wrote in 1807 that Dalton's vision deficiency was due to the lack of one of the vibrating systems. His hypothesis was close to the reality.

After Dalton's death, his eyes were examined as he requested. The eyes were normal in every way that could be determined at that time. The color receiving cones could not be seen, so no difference was found in them.

Recall that Dalton also had a difference in his vision based on the source of light. Today's spectrum studies show that candlelight has a high red content, which would alter a protanope's vision while only slightly changing the perception of a person with normal vision.

Another part of Dalton's research has been confirmed: More males are affected by the condition than females. The gene for defective color vision is carried on the X chromosome. Males have X-Y pairs and females X-X. A female would have to have the defective gene on both X chromosomes, while a male needs only one to have the condition. Therefore, color deficiency is more common in males. Females can be carriers of the gene without having the condition.

Dalton settled in Manchester and began to have a regular schedule. Each day, he got up early and wrote the weather conditions in his meteorology notebook. Then he went to the building of the Manchester Literary and Philosophical Society, where he spent the morning teaching his students. In the afternoon, he performed experiments in the laboratory that was assigned to him in the Society house.

In 1801, he published a book that seems completely out of character for the man we know as a chemist. He wrote *Elements of English Grammar: or a new system of grammatical instruction for the use of schools and academies.* He wrote it because he felt that the current grammar books were not good enough. He wanted a grammar system that was logical and easy to teach. He wrote to Elihu Robinson about his new project, "I think they [other grammar books] are all very bad, or I should not have been at the trouble to write one principally for my own use. I am now in the practice of teaching it, and find it the most intelligible to my young people of any they have met with."

Dalton's scientific bent is revealed in his grammar book, which states, "Grammatically speaking, therefore, there are three times, present, past and future; though strictly and mathematically speaking, we can admit only two, past and future."

This was Dalton's only book outside of the scientific arena. His papers over the next few years would seal his reputation as a foremost scientist.

Fascination with Gases

The city of Manchester, where Dalton lived and taught beginning in 1793, was at the forefront of the Industrial Revolution. As the weaving and spinning industries moved out of cottages and into factories, Manchester became a thriving textile center. The population expanded from 17,000 in 1758 to more than 70,000 in 1801. Located about one hundred miles north of London, Manchester became the second-largest city in the country and rivaled London in its economic power.

Cotton from America was unloaded each day at Manchester's docks, and it was swept into the steam-driven spinning machines and looms. All around Manchester, people could hear the sound of steam engines.

The combination of his meteorological work and, probably, the constant reminder of the power of steam led Dalton to his first great discovery. The breakthrough could properly be placed in the field of physics, but the idea demonstrates Dalton's thinking about particles.

In his first book, *Meteorological Observations and Essays*, Dalton had written a section about water vapor. He stated that water vapor existed as a separate gas in the gases of air, not chemically combined with them.

After his paper on color vision, he read to the Manchester Lit & Phil his paper "Experiments and Observations to determine whether the Quantity of Rain and Dew is equal to the Quantity of Water carried off by the Rivers and raised by Evaporation; with an Enquiry into the Origin of Springs." The long title summarizes his working hypothesis: Does the water in rivers and from springs come solely from rain and dew?

Other scientists had pondered this question, but Dalton decided to measure it as nearly as he could. Today, we understand the process as the water cycle and accept it, but in Dalton's day it was a controversial concept.

Some believed that springs pulled water from subterranean reservoirs or filled up with seawater filtrated through soil. Dalton's premise was that all the water needed for springs came from rainfall and dew.

His first step was to determine total rainfall for the country. He took rain measurements from about thirty places, averaged them by county, and found an average for the entire country. The average rainfall he calculated was thirty-one inches. For the amount of dew, he increased an estimate by an earlier scientist, Stephen Hale, and arrived at five inches.

At this point in the paper, he added a footnote stating that water vapor is "an elastic fluid *sui generis* [a class alone], diffusible in the atmosphere but forming no chemical compound with it." He went on to say that water vapor content is dependent on temperature and that water is present in the atmosphere at all times.

Dalton described his method of determining dew point, or what he called "the extreme temperature of vapour." By putting cold water in a glass and sometimes lowering the temperature of the water by adding saltpeter, he observed the temperature when dew formed on the outside of the glass.

Once he calculated the rainfall and dew amounts, he needed to know the flow of the rivers. He used measurements from other scientists. They had determined flow by timing a weighted rod floating past two points and multiplying the elapsed time by the cross-section area of the river. Dalton discovered that the Thames River accounted for a little more than one-twenty-fifth of all rainfall. Comparing other rivers and their flow to the Thames, he calculated that their flow left twenty-three inches of rain that were not carried by the rivers. Where did all that rain end up?

Evaporation was the next water cycle component that Dalton measured. He mentioned experiments of others but then described his own. He filled a cylinder with earth. A tube from the top would drain off surface rainwater and be measured. A tube at the bottom would measure the amount of water that percolated through the soil. A nearby rain gauge indicated total rainfall, so adding the measurements of the two tubes would provide a difference that would be equal to the amount of water lost by evaporation. With these four measurements—water in the rivers, water percolated, water evaporated, and in water as dew—Dalton arrived at the average amount of rainfall measured: thirty-one inches. Therefore, he concluded that springs are replenished by rainfall and dew.

Dalton's explanation provided a skeleton view of the water cycle as we know it today. But his study of water vapor in air had just begun. He also conducted studies of heat.

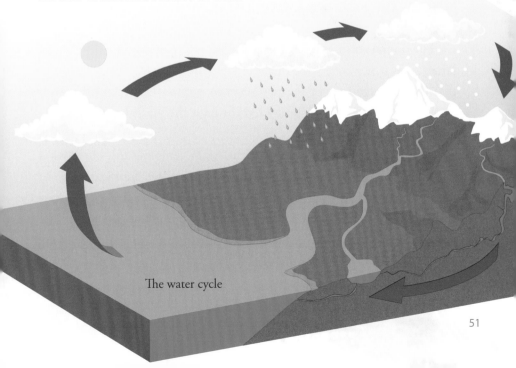

The water cycle

His next paper for the Lit & Phil contradicted a paper by famed scientist Count Rumford. In a 1798 paper, Rumford had asserted that heat transfer in water occurs by convection and that water does not conduct heat. Dalton suspected that conduction did play a part and set up experiments to prove his point.

In today's definitions, convection is heat transfer by the actual movement of heated material. Steam in a radiator or heated air passing through a room heats the entire room by movement of warm currents. Conduction depends on the collision of heated particles to transfer heat. A spoon placed in a hot bowl of soup becomes warm because the atoms of the soup are vibrating faster, and they pass some of that energy to the atoms of the spoon, raising its temperature.

In Rumford's experiments, he put ice at the bottom of a jar and poured water on top. Only a little more ice was melted by boiling water than by 42° water. Since the 42° water was at its maximum density (as others had determined), as the water near the ice cooled, it should rise by convection and 42° water should fill in its place because the 42° water would be more dense. But Rumford thought this was not true, believing instead that each layer of water would stay its own temperature.

For one experiment, Dalton put cold water in a glass above a container of warm water, with thermometers in both sections. He found that the temperatures of the two sections approached each other over time. The heat had been conducted through the glass that divided the two containers.

Dalton filled a glass with water at room temperature. He stuck a red-hot poker into the water. Over an hour's time, he measured the temperature at the top, middle, and bottom of the glass. The chart shows his findings: The top number is the original temperature of the water. The second is immediately after putting the hot poker in—the top is 180° and the bottom is 47°.

Time	At Top	Middle	Bottom
Before the Poker was immersed			47°
	180°		47°
5 min	100°	60°	47.5°
20 min	70°	60°	49°
1 hour	55°		52°

Dalton's statements in this paper show that he was already thinking of matter as particles. He demonstrated that heat transfer in water occurs from conduction, in conjunction with convection.

Many scientists thought that just as salt dissolves in water, water vapor dissolves in air. This explanation would clarify why water "precipitates" out as the air cools, forming dew. However, scientists had shown that water also evaporates in a vacuum, thereby "dissolving" into nothing.

Isaac Newton had named liquid vapor as a "sort of air" in his "Proof of Boyle's Law." Robert Boyle had stated a law based on his observations of gases: As the pressure on a gas decreases, the volume increases, and vice versa. The Kinetic Theory of Gases—that the particles are always moving—had not yet been developed. So neither Boyle nor Newton described the gas particles in motion. Following their ideas of mixed gases, gases of one kind would fit in the spaces of the other gas.

On June 27, 1800, Dalton read a paper that he had written en-

titled "Experiments and observations on the Heat and Cold produced by the mechanical condensation and rarefaction [expansion] of air." In this paper, Dalton noted that different experimental results can be obtained based on the amount of water vapor in the air. He compared results with dry air and with wet or humid air. He wrote about experiments "in a cold morning last winter" and in "a dyer's store where the temperature was about 100°, and the air abounded with vapor in the transparent state." Dalton reported that gases expand one-tenth of their volume for every 50°.

Dalton's results in this paper were not perfect. His experimental technique was not always the best. But his conclusions were good, and we can see that he was learning more about chemistry all the time.

Just before the presentation of this paper, Dalton had been elected secretary of the Manchester Literary and Philosophical Society. He served in this capacity for the next nine years. The job included correspondence, editorial work on the Lit & Phil's publications, and business activities for the Society. The ratio of scientific papers to the literary ones increased after Dalton's election, probably because of his influence. He is listed as presenting 117 papers over the years of his membership.

In 1801, Dalton wrote four essays that were first printed in *Nich-*

olson's Journal and then in the *Memoirs of the Manchester Literary and Philosophical Society* in 1802. The titles of the four essays show the comprehensive nature of the work:

1. On the Constitution of Mixed Gases.
2. On the Force of Steam of Vapor and Other Liquids in Different Temperatures, Both in a Torricellian Vacuum and in Air.
3. On Evaporation.
4. On the Expansion of Gases by Heat.

The dominant view of gases at the time was that expressed by Isaac Newton. He saw gas particles in a static state unless they were forced to move by repulsive forces between the particles. Some scientists believed that particles in gases were surrounded by a cloud of caloric—an imponderable material that produced heat (or, put another way, an invisible fluid not having weight). The caloric cloud could be compressed, but it filled the space between particles.

Dalton rejected the idea that gases in the atmosphere chemically combined, and so he considered them to be physically mixed. Still, how would gases of different weights stay uniformly mixed and not settle into layers? The possibility that each gas particle repels other similar particles as well as different particles was considered. Even if that were true, the end result would be stratification.

At the beginning of the essay, Dalton stated Boyle's Law, one of the basic gas laws learned by beginning chemistry students today. In Dalton's words: "The density of elastic fluids is exactly as the compressing force, all other circumstances alike." He pointed out that an experimenter must be careful to avoid water vapor in other gases because it would skew the results.

Dalton's alternative idea came to be called Dalton's Law of Partial Pressures. As he stated it, "When two elastic fluids [gases], denoted by A and B, are mixed together, there is no mutual repulsion among their particles; that is, the particles of A do not repel those of B, as they do one another. Consequently, the pressure or whole weight upon any one particle arises solely from those of its own kind."

In modern terms, we say that the total pressure in a mixed gas is the sum of the individual partial pressures. In mathematical terms, $P = p1 + p2 + p3 + \ldots$. We know the law works because the atoms or molecules of a gas are constantly moving. Their kinetic energy produces pressure.

In the second essay, Dalton shared his belief that there "can scarcely be a doubt entertained respecting the reducibility of all elastic fluids, of whatever kind, into liquids." About twenty years later, Michael Faraday proved this true by liquefying several gases. Dalton distinguished between vapor and gases. The materials that had not yet been liquefied, he called gases.

Some of the experiments that Dalton noted dealt with vapor pressure over liquids. He wrote, "The object of the present Essay is to determine the utmost force that certain vapours, as that from water, can exert at different temperatures." Dalton added that this set of experiments had arisen from the consideration of work done by steam, which was evident all around him in Manchester. In his conclusion, he wrote, "when the temperature of a liquid is increased, the force of vapor from it is increased with amazing rapidity, the increments of elasticity forming a kind of geometrical progression, to the arithmetical increments of heat."

In his third essay, Dalton included a list of experiments that measured the time for water and other liquids to turn to vapor, by boiling or evaporation. He also demonstrated that ice does evaporate.

Besides Boyle's Law, students today learn Charles's Law: At constant pressure, gases expand in a linear fashion as the temperature rises. All gases expand at the same rate. Some French experimenters had found widely varying amounts, and they published their results. Dalton realized that the contradictory results were due to water vapor in the gases. In his fourth essay, "On the Expansion of Gases by Heat" [elastic fluids is the term for Gases in Dalton's time], he investigated a number of gases, including air, hydrogen, oxygen, nitrogen, and carbon dioxide. Unaware of the statement of Charles's Law, Dalton stated it in his own way, "All elastic fluids expand the same quantity by heat."

Dalton's papers stirred up controversy. His blind friend from Kendal, John Gough, believed that air was a compound. So he attacked Dalton's hypothesis vigorously. Dalton carefully pointed out some mistakes in Gough's thinking, taking care not to humiliate his former tutor.

Dalton's friend William Henry wrote to him in 1804, stating, "In the discussions . . . which took place in this Society [Lit & Phil], on your several papers, the doctrine was opposed by almost every member interested in such subjects, and by no one more strenuously than myself." However, by the time Henry wrote the letter, he had become convinced of the validity of Dalton's ideas. In his own experiments, he discovered what is now called Henry's Law: The weight of a gas dissolved in a liquid is directly proportional to the pressure of the gas above the liquid. Henry said that Dalton's hypothesis was "better adapted than any former one, for explaining the relation of mixed gases to each other, and especially the connection between gases and water."

His work with gases had strengthened Dalton's vision of particles. Some of the conclusions led to more questions. Striving to answer these questions would lead him to his ultimate scientific achievement.

The Atomic Theory Is Born

John Dalton was not the first person to suggest that matter is made up of atoms. The idea of atoms as indivisible particles goes back more than 2,000 years to the time of Democritus, the Greek philosopher. Democritus said that you can break a dirt clod into smaller pieces and those pieces into even smaller ones, but eventually you get down to particles that cannot be broken down anymore. He gave these particles the name "atoms" from a Greek word that means indivisible, uncuttable.

Greek philosopher Aristotle was born in 384 B.C. He believed that there were four elements—air, water, fire, and earth—and that everything came from these elements. His ideas were the accepted science for almost 2,000 years.

In the Middle Ages, people began to question Aristotle's ideas. Alchemists tried to purify matter and turn such metals as lead into such precious metals as gold and silver. They never could turn lead into gold, but they did develop new methods to purify metals and make new chemical compounds.

A French scientist, Pierre Gassendi, went back to the old idea of atoms in his writings in the 1600s. Sir Isaac Newton, who is famous for his gravity theory, agreed with Pierre that all things are composed of atoms. In Newton's book *Opticks*, published a century before Dalton, Newton wrote, "It seems probable to me that God in the beginning formed matter in *solid, massy, hard, impenetrable, movable* particles of such *size* and *figures* . . . and that these primitive particles being solids, are incomparably harder than any porous bodies compounded of them; even so hard as never to wear or break in pieces."

However, Newton and English chemist Robert Boyle thought that some basic matter existed that changed to become different elements. They conceived primary particles that were identical and formed the various elements by different combinations.

Sir Isaac
Newton

Over the next hundred years, more and more scientists began to agree that matter was composed of atoms. French chemist Antoine Lavoisier proposed that if "we apply the term *elements* or *principles of bodies*, to express our idea of the last point which analysis is capable of reaching, we must admit as elements, all the substances into which are capable, by any means, to reduce bodies during decomposition." He published a list of elements in 1789. Chemists later showed that some of Lavoisier's elements were compounds that he hadn't been able to separate, but his list made chemists think about elements and atoms. Lavoisier was beheaded during the French Revolution in 1794.

John Dalton carried out his own experiments to study elements and atoms. His meteorological and gas studies led him to think of particles. Early in 1803, Dalton wrote a letter to his brother about his recent work. "I have been, as usual, fully engaged in all my leisure hours, in the pursuit of chemical and philosophical enquires. Even my Christmas vacation was taken up in this way; indeed I have had considerable success of late in this line, having got into a track that has not been much trod in before."

By October 1803, people learned about some of Dalton's work. In a paper read to the Lit & Phil, he detailed experiments with the solubilities of gases in water. In his experiments, he had found that hydrogen, the lightest gas, does not dissolve easily in water. But a heavier gas such as carbon dioxide is soluble in water. He asked the important question "Why does water not admit its bulk of every kind of gas alike? . . . This question I have duly considered, and though I am not yet able to satisfy myself completely, I am nearly persuaded that the circumstance depends upon the weight and number of the ultimate particles of the several gases: Those whose particles are lightest and single being least absorbable and the others more according as they increase in weight and complexity." For the first time, Dalton began to consider the weight of atoms.

At the end of this paper, he attached a "Table of the relative weights of the ultimate particles of gaseous and other bodies."

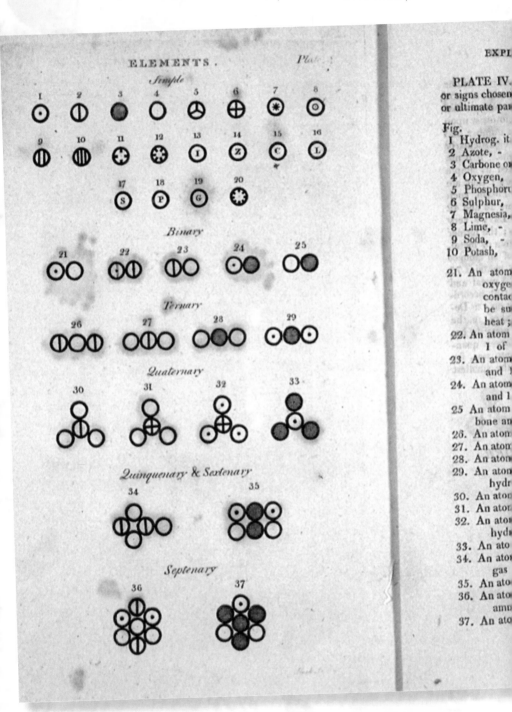

Dalton's "Table of the relative weights of the ultimate particles of gaseous and other bodies"

THE PLATES.   219

contains the arbitrary marks
...e several chemical elements

Fig.
11 Strontites - - - 46
12 Barytes - - - - 68
13 Iron - - - - - 38
14 Zinc - - - - - 56
15 Copper - - - - 56
16 Lead - - - - - 95
17 Silver - - - - - 100
18 Platina - - - - 100
19 Gold - - - - - 140
20 Mercury - - - - 167

steam, composed of 1 of
...ogen, retained in physical
affinity, and supposed to
common atmosphere of
...ight = - - - - 8
...mposed of 1 of azote and
- - - - - - - 6
, composed of 1 of azote
- - - - - - - 12
composed of 1 of carbone
- - - - - - 6
...de composed of 1 of car-
- - - - - - 12
...e, 2 azote + 1 oxygen - 17
1 azote + 2 oxygen - - 19
...id, 1 carbone + 2 oxygen 19
hydrogen, 1 carbone + 2
- - - - - - - 7
...acid, 1 azote + 3 oxygen 26
...cid, 1 sulphur + 3 oxygen 34
...d hydrogen, 1 sulphur + 3.
- - - - - - 16
...carbone + 1 hydrogen - 16
...id, 1 nitric acid + 1 nitrous
- - - - - - 31
...id, 2 carbone + 2 water - 26
ammonia, 1 nitric acid + 1
- - - - - - 33
...lcohol + 1 carbonic acid - 35

How would you determine the weight of something you can't see? Notice that Dalton calculated relative weights, meaning weights in relation to one another. He knew that hydrogen was the lightest "ultimate particle" known at the time, so he assigned it a weight of one. By measuring the amounts of other elements in compounds with hydrogen, he devised the table. Many of the amounts were off from what we know today, but this was the first attempt to weigh atoms. The proposition that atoms have a specific weight led Dalton to his greatest theory and prompted other chemists to focus on the atom as a reality. Today, we see an atomic weight listed on the Periodic Table and accept it as a characteristic of each element.

From December 1803 to January 1804, Dalton was in London for a lecture series at the Royal Institution. The Royal Institution had been founded in 1799 by fifty-eight men who gave the institution the mission of promoting education and industrial progress. The institution never quite reached its intended goal of educating the public as a whole, but it became an important research center. Lectures by scientists from around Britain and the world were highlights of the year and a means of propagating new developments in science.

Dalton's lectures covered mechanics, electricity, magnetism, his color-blindness, astronomy, sound, and his experiments on heat and the constitution of mixed gases. For his lectures, Dalton received eighty guineas. While many noted Dalton as a poor lecturer with a gruff and accented voice and an uninspiring style, others were excited by his demonstrations. His straightforward teaching contrasted vividly with Sir Humphry Davy's charismatic delivery.

In August 1804, Dalton received a visitor from Edinburgh, Scotland. Thomas Thomson had attended University of Edinburgh with Dalton's friend William Henry, and both men had begun studying medicine. Scottish chemist Joseph Black was conducting groundbreaking work at the time, and his ideas captured the imagination of both Henry and Thomson. Henry was unable to finish medical school, as he was called back to the family pharmacy business in Manchester. Thomson did finish medical school. He wrote science articles for *Encyclopaedia Britannica*, published in Edinburgh, and wrote a chemistry textbook, *System of Chemistry*. Thomson also began a teaching laboratory, the first in Great Britain.

Dalton, Thomson, and Henry discussed experiments on mixed gases, on the chemical composition of what we now call methane (CH^4) and ethane (C^2H^6). Dalton had recently experimented on these gases, substantiating his idea of chemical compositions being in ratios of whole numbers.

After Thomson returned to Scotland, he published a third edition of *System of Chemistry*. He added a section about Dalton's work on the relative weights of gaseous atoms and even extended the method to metal compounds and acids and bases.

About the time that Thomson's book came out, Dalton delivered a set of lectures in Edinburgh and Glasgow. In the introduction to his first lecture, Dalton said, "My attention has been directed for several years past, with considerable assiduity, to the subjects of *heat*, of *elastic fluids*, of the *primary elements* of bodies, and the *mode of their combinations*. In the prosecution of these studies several new and important facts and observations have occurred. I have been enabled to reduce a number of apparently anomalous facts to general laws." Dalton, with his desire for simplicity, had assembled a multitude of known chemical facts into a few universal laws.

Dalton enjoyed visiting Scotland, and when he returned, he began a new book—his most famous work. He called it *New System of Chemical Philosophy*, which was based on his Scottish lectures and the ideas he had discussed with Thomson. Volume 1, Part 1 was published in June 1808 at a price of seven shillings. Volume 1, Part 2 came out in 1810, and Volume 2, Part 1 was printed in 1827. The second part of Volume 2 was never finished. However, this book contains the ideas that we call the Atomic Theory.

The dedication of the book was as follows: "To the Professors of the Universities, and other Residents, of Edinburgh and Glasgow, who gave their attention and encouragement to the Lectures on Heat and Chemical Elements, Delivered to those Cities in 1807; and to the Members of the Literary and Philosophical Society of Manchester, who have uniformly promoted his researches: this Work is respectfully inscribed by the Author."

Two-thirds of the book deals with the idea of heat—or "caloric," as Dalton called it. He wrote about different theories of heat and how it interacts with matter. In Section 7, he compared the heat-conducting capacity of different materials and wrote, "This power of conducting heat varies greatly, according to the nature of the subject: in general, metals, and those bodies which are good conductors of electricity, are likewise good conductors of heat; and vice versa."

In another section, he experimented with ice and water and their densities. He stated the facts he had discovered, including that "the specific gravity of ice is less than that of water in the ratio of 92 to 100." He found that the density of water is greatest at 38°; it expands and becomes less

dense both below and above that temperature. He also provided an observation that when ice forms, the shoots (as he called them) develop at angles of 60° and 120°. Today we recognize that this is true because of the angles between hydrogen and oxygen atoms in the water molecule.

Finally, in Chapter III, Dalton entered Atomic Theory territory. He stated the Law of Conservation of Matter, much as Antoine Lavoisier had proclaimed it. "Chemical analysis and synthesis go no farther than to the separation of particles one from another, and to their reunion," Dalton wrote. "No new creation or destruction of matter is within the reach of chemical agency. We might as well attempt to introduce a new planet into the solar system, or to annihilate one already in existence; as to create or destroy a particle of hydrogen."

When a chemical reaction takes place, atoms combine and form a completely different substance. For example, water looks nothing like the gases of hydrogen and oxygen that it comes from. But Dalton believed that the hydrogen atoms in water still weigh the same as in the gas. He said that chemical reactions only shuffle the atoms, but do not change their basic character, such as weight.

The next thing Dalton wanted to figure out was relative weights of atoms. How could he do that? He couldn't even see an atom. "Now it is one great object of this work, to show the importance and advantage of ascertaining *the relative weights of the ultimate particles, both of simple and compound bodies* [molecules], *the number of simple elementary particles which constitute one compound particle, and the number of less compound particles which enter into the formation of one more compound particle.*" True to his character, Dalton took the direct route. He imagined two atoms combining and tried to decide what would happen:

If there are two bodies, A and B, which are disposed to combine, the following is the order in which the combinations may take place, beginning with the most simple:

> 1 atom of A + 1 atom of B = 1 atom of C, binary.
> 1 atom of A + 2 atoms of B = 1 atom of D, ternary.
> 2 atoms of A + 1 atom of B = 1 atom of E, ternary.
> 1 atom of A + 3 atoms of B = 1 atom of F, quaternary.
> 3 atoms of A + 1 atom of B = 1 atom of G, quaternary.
> etc., etc.

Dalton's system in some ways seems intuitive to us, as does the existence of atoms. His atoms—C, D, E, F, G—are all what we call molecules. But this list of possibilities leads to other ideas. Dalton continued:

The following general rules may be adopted as guides in all our investigations respecting chemical synthesis.

1st   When only one combination of two bodies can be obtained, it must be presumed to be a binary one, unless some cause appear to the contrary.

2d   When two combinations are observed, they must be presumed to be a binary and a ternary.

3d   When three combinations are obtained, we may expect one to be binary, and the other two ternary.

4th   When four combinations are observed, we should expect one binary, two ternary, and one quaternary, etc.

5th   A binary compound should always be specifically heavier than the mere mixture of its two ingredients.

6th   A ternary compound should be specifically heavier than the mixture of a binary and a simple, which would, if combined, constitute it; etc.

7th   The above rules and observations equally apply, when two bodies, such as C and D, D and E, etc. are combined.

From these rules, Dalton concluded that water is a binary molecule combined of one atom of hydrogen and one of oxygen. He also thought that ammonia was one atom of hydrogen and one of nitrogen. We know that water has two atoms of hydrogen and one of oxygen, and ammonia has one of nitrogen and three of hydrogen. Dalton's thinking of these molecules as binary came partly from his belief that similar atoms would repel each other to the point of not combining, or at least to be as far apart as possible in a molecule. He also thought that a molecule with two atoms would be most stable and, therefore, most likely. The understanding of bond angles would have to wait another 150 years.

Dalton decided to make a table of relative weights. He knew that hydrogen seemed to be the lightest atom, so he gave it the weight of 1. He believed that water was one atom of hydrogen bonded to one atom of oxygen. In analysis, there seemed to be seven times (by weight) more oxygen than hydrogen. Therefore, he gave oxygen a relative weight of 7.

For ammonia, Dalton believed that one atom of hydrogen combined with one of nitrogen, giving nitrogen a relative weight of 5.

He analyzed many compounds to determine the relative weights of their components and set up a table of relative weights. He wrote the table in his notebook.

While studying two compounds, Dalton began to think about how atoms formed compounds. Nitric acid contains one atom of nitrogen and one of oxygen. A different compound also has nitrogen and oxygen. Nitrous oxide has two atoms of nitrogen and one of oxygen. Two other compounds that contain the same atoms are carbon monoxide and carbon dioxide. Carbon monoxide has one atom of carbon and one of oxygen. Carbon dioxide is one atom of carbon and two of oxygen. With these results, Dalton decided that atoms always combine in whole number ratios. You get either one or two atoms of nitrogen for one atom of oxygen, but never one and a half atoms.

In chemistry books today, the Atomic Theory is stated in four items:

1. Each element contains atoms that are indivisible.

2. Atoms cannot be created or destroyed.

3. The atoms of each element are totally alike, in weight, volume, and chemical properties. Atoms of different elements have different characteristics.

4. In chemical combinations of different elements, atoms bond in simple definite numbers.

Earlier scientists, such as Robert Boyle and Sir Isaac Newton, had believed in an untouchable, undefined matter that changed to become different elements. That is like saying that the letter *b* is sometimes *b* and sometimes *c*. Dalton stated that *b* is always *b* whether it is joined with -*at* for *bat* or with -*ad* for *bad*. He made the basic unit of matter, the atom, a reality to chemists, and this changed their focus. The Atomic Theory enabled chemists to visualize atoms, molecules, and changes during reactions.

One corollary to the theory is called the Law of Definite Proportions. This law states that elements combine always in the same numbers in a compound. For example, salt is always one atom of sodium and one of chlorine, not sometimes two chlorines.

Dalton's theory gave numbers and quantity to chemical facts that had been observed for years. His quantitative results and the system of relative weights added a mathematical aspect to chemistry that it had not had before. The theory married the results of theoretical chemistry to that of the practical chemist who worked in industry.

Controversy and New Symbols

Once Dalton's Atomic Theory was published, controversy arose. Many scientists were willing to accept the sections on definite proportions in chemical reactions but not the rest of it.

Sir Humphry Davy, one of Britain's leading scientists, rejected Dalton's theory. Thomas Thomson, the chemist who had first published the theory, stated that he tried to persuade Davy of its validity: "In the autumn of 1807 I had a long conversation with him [Davy] at the Royal Institution, but could not convince him there was any truth in the hypothesis. . . . After dinner . . . Dr. Wollaston, Mr. Davy and myself . . . sat about an hour and a half together, and our whole conversation was about the atomic theory. Dr. Wollaston was a convert as well as myself; and we tried to convince Davy of the inaccuracy of his opinions; but, so far from being convinced, he went away, if possible, more prejudiced against it than ever."

Davy's biggest objection was that the theory called for different atoms for each element. Several elements had been discovered by Davy, including sodium, potassium, calcium, and others. But he still believed in an ultimate particle that would be the same for every element.

When Dalton visited London in 1810 to present lectures at the Royal Institution, Davy recognized Dalton's scientific accomplishments enough to suggest that he apply for membership in the Royal Society. Dalton didn't apply, and it has been speculated that he couldn't afford the fee. But also, he would have to request admittance, and perhaps he was too humble to do so and it would interfere with his Quaker beliefs to put himself forward. In 1822, he became a member when his friends managed to waive the requirement for him to petition for membership.

Sir Humphry Davy

In a series of experiments on oxalic acid, Thomson obtained strong evidence in favor of Dalton's theory. He synthesized and decomposed this compound—what we would call an organic compound—and used Dalton's ideas to determine the weight of each element.

William Hyde Wollaston was also experimenting with oxalic acid, as well as other compounds, and was close to discovering the Law of Definite Proportions before Dalton did. He added a structural concept to Dalton's theory: "that when our views are sufficiently extended, to enable us to reason with precision concerning the proportions of elementary atoms, we shall find the arithmetical relation alone will not be sufficient to explain their mutual action, and that we shall be obliged to acquire a geometrical conception of their relative arrangement in all three dimensions of solid extension."

French chemist Claude Berthollet was skeptical about Dalton's Atomic Theory. He struggled with the idea of definite proportions because of his experiences in Egypt. As part of Napoleon's expedition, Berthollet had discovered a salt lake in Egypt that had deposits of soda around the edge. Analyses showed that the soda came from a reaction between the salt and limestone layers at the bottom of the lake—a complete opposite of the usual reaction of soda (sodium carbonate) and calcium chloride to form salt and limestone (calcium carbonate). Berthollet theorized that the heavy concentration of salt forced the reaction in the opposite direction. He had discovered what we call an equilibrium reaction:

$$CaCl^2 + Na^2CO^3 \leftrightarrow CaCO^3 + 2NaCl$$

This discovery led Berthollet to believe that matter combined in variable and indefinite proportions. Therefore, he rejected Dalton's ideas.

A protégé of Berthollet actually discovered a relation that strongly supported Dalton's theory. Joseph Gay-Lussac studied gases. He found that simple relations existed in the behavior of gases. For example, regardless of what gas was tested, equal volumes expanded equally with heat and decompressed equally with pressure. Gaseous acids neutralized equal volumes of gaseous bases. He also found that gases reacted with each other in whole number ratios. Gay-Lussac wrote, "These ratios by volume are not observed with solid or liquid substances, nor when we consider weights, and they form a new proof that it is only in the gaseous state that substances are in the same circumstances and obey regular laws."

Gay-Lussac's contribution came to be called the Law of Combining Volumes. This law and Dalton's Atomic Theory would lead to Amedeo Avogadro's hypothesis that equal volumes of gases contain equal number of atoms. The regular laws that the gases were demonstrating fit perfectly with Dalton's Atomic Theory.

Dalton rejected Gay-Lussac's Law of Combining Volumes. In an appendix for Part 2 of *New System*, Dalton wrote: "his [Gay-Lussac's] notion of measures is analogous to mine of atoms; and if it could be proved that all elastic fluids [gases] have the same number of atoms in the same volume, or numbers that are 1, 2, 3, &c. the two hypotheses would be the same, except that mine is universal, and his applies only to elastic fluids."

Joseph Gay-Lussac

Dalton's rejection was based on his belief that equal volumes of gas could not contain the same number of atoms. In his experiments with gases, Dalton had found several instances in which heavier reactants form a lighter product. For example, the reaction of hydrogen and oxygen, a heavier gas, produces water vapor, a lighter gas than oxygen. Dalton believed that this proved that a lighter gas must have fewer particles than a heavier gas. He didn't know that hydrogen and oxygen gases contain molecules of two atoms of each element. In fact, he believed that repulsion would forbid a hydrogen molecule with two atoms of hydrogen bound together. So when two volumes of ammonia were produced when one volume of nitrogen reacted with three volumes of hydrogen, Dalton concluded that each volume of ammonia must contain only half the particles of the nitrogen volume.

In 1811, Avogadro published a work that actually reconciled Dalton's and Gay-Lussac's work. He hypothesized the two-atom molecule for some gases, and he proposed that equal volumes of gas contain an equal number of particles. However, his work was not widely circulated, and so the acceptance of Avogadro's number (the number of particles in a liter of gas) had to wait for a while.

A Swedish chemist, Jons Jacob Berzelius, stirred up more controversy. He had studied work by J. B. Richter, which showed that a unit weight of acid neutralized an equivalent weight of base. Richter had determined equivalent weights for a number of acids and bases. These equivalents added to the idea that compounds always form in definite amounts. The hypothesis led Berzelius to begin an exhaustive examination of compounds. When he first heard about Dalton's Atomic Theory, he was impressed. He wrote: "such a doctrine of the composition of compounds would so illuminate the province of affinity, that supposing Dalton's hypothesis be found correct, we should have to look upon it as the greatest advance that chemistry has ever yet made in its development into a science. I have no knowledge whatever of how Dalton developed his theory and on what experiments he has based his thesis, and hence cannot judge whether they modify it in a greater or lesser degree."

Berzelius tried to get a copy of Dalton's *A New System of Chemical Philosophy*, but he was unable to do so for a couple of years because of ongoing wars in Europe. When he finally got one, sent to him by Dalton, he was disappointed. He wrote: "Never has a present given me such pleasure as this one did at first. I have been able only to skim through the book in haste, but I will not conceal that I was surprised to see how the author had disappointed my hopes."

Actually, Berzelius had come up with what he called a corpuscular theory, which

Jons Jacob Berzelius

was close to Dalton's theory. In his meticulous examination of chemical compounds, he began to divide chemicals into two groups—those that were electropositive and those electronegative. His continued studies eventually electrified Dalton's atoms, laying the groundwork for the understanding of chemical bonds in future years.

One of the biggest contentions between Dalton and Berzelius was the shape of atoms. Berzelius saw all atoms as spherical and the same size. Dalton would not speculate on a relationship between size and shape of atoms. He tended to see atoms as not the same size, but he did believe that all atoms—whatever their shape—were surrounded by a spherical atmosphere of heat. Part of this discussion was based on studies of crystals, which show a regular pattern. For Berzelius, that implied equal sizes of atoms. The jump from atoms combining into molecules to the structure of those molecules had not been proven. Structural chemistry would come in a few more years.

Dalton and Berzelius also disagreed about chemical symbols. Dalton designated atoms and molecules with round symbols. For example, hydrogen was a circle with a dot in it, carbon was a solid circle, and oxygen was an open circle. He would write carbon dioxide as ○●○, not ○○●. His system implied a structure that had not been proven. However, he wrote, "When three or more particles of elastic fluids are combined together in one, it is to be supposed that the particles of the same kind repel each other, and therefore take their stations accordingly." Dalton's system did reinforce the idea of atoms combining into molecules because each atom was designated by a symbol. However, the system was hard for printers to incorporate into books and had to be memorized.

Berzelius devised his own system of symbols. In fact, it is the basic system that we use today. He proposed using letters to show elements and to write these as a combination to show a molecule. The reasoning for his plan was the same as Dalton's. Berzelius wrote that "the new signs . . . are destined solely to facilitate the expression of chemical proportions."

Berzelius was not the first to use letters to show chemicals, but his system was the one finally accepted by chemists. Dalton did not accept it. As he wrote in a letter, "Berzelius' symbols are horrifying. A young student of chemistry might as soon learn Hebrew as make himself acquainted with him. They appear like a chaos of atoms." To another person, Dalton asserted, "I do not, however, approve of his adopting and defending the chemical symbols of Berzelius, which appear to me equally to perplex the adepts of science, to discourage the learner, as well as to cloud the beauty and simplicity of the atomic theory."

Any chemistry student who has struggled to learn the symbols proposed by Berzelius can agree that they can be confusing. Imagine using Au for gold and K for potassium. These symbols came from the Latin names for these elements. Still, Dalton's system would also be a lot to memorize and much harder to write than the current system.

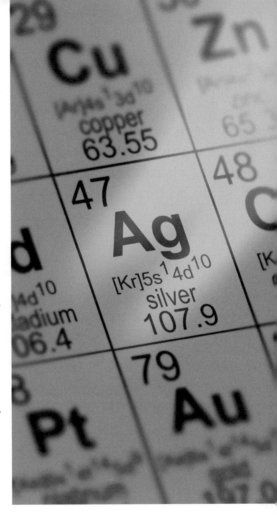

Dalton was still living in Manchester, although he no longer taught at New College. Conditions at the college deteriorated because of fewer students until 1800, when Dalton and other tutors resigned. The school eventually relocated to York. Dalton continued to support himself with private tutoring.

A special friend of Dalton's was Reverend William Johns. The two had taught at New College together. Johns, his wife, and two daughters lived at 25 George Street. Years later, the older daughter recalled the story of how Dalton came to live with them: "As my mother was standing at her parlour window one evening towards dusk, she saw

Mr. Dalton passing on the other side of the street, and on opening the widow, he crossed over and greeted her. 'Mr. Dalton,' said she, 'how is it that you seldom come to see us?' 'Why, I don't know,' he replied; 'but I have a mind to come and live with you.' My mother thought at first that he was in jest, but finding that he really meant what he said, she asked him to call again the next day, after she should have consulted my father. Accordingly, he came and took possession of the only bed-room at liberty, which he continued to occupy for nearly thirty years."

Miss Johns tells of Dalton's schedule and lifestyle. He typically awoke at about eight o'clock, walked to his laboratory at the Lit & Phil (about two minutes away) and lit the fire, ate breakfast, and returned to the lab. After lunch, he chatted with the family and then spent the afternoon in the laboratory again. He returned to the house for tea at five o'clock. He spent some of this time with his students. After supper, Dalton and the family chatted, and Dalton and Mr. Johns smoked their pipes. On most days, he also went to a nearby library to read the newspapers. On Thursday afternoons, Dalton joined a group of friends at the Dog and Partridge, where they played a game of bowls and had tea.

In later reminiscences, Miss Johns said, "I may mention that my sister and myself never left home, be the hour ever so untimely, that he did not see us into the coach and safe off. But not only to us, to the servants also did he pay the same kind attention on their annual visits to see their friends."

Dalton's work on the Atomic Theory from about 1803 to 1808 proved to be his greatest accomplishment. He continued to write some papers, but they did not have the insight of his Atomic Theory. In 1839, the Royal Society rejected a paper he submitted because other scientists had done a better job of presenting the material.

Inside London's Science Museum

Atoms were so real to Dalton that he asked a friend, Peter Ewart, to make some wooden ball models. In a paper on the analysis of different sugars, he wrote, "My friend, Mr. Ewart, at my suggestion made me a number of equal balls, about an inch in diameter, about thirty years ago; they have been in use ever since, I occasionally showing them to my students." Three of his ball and stick models can be seen in the Science Museum of London. H. E. Roscoe, who wrote a biography about John Dalton, quipped, "Atoms are round bits of wood invented by Mr. Dalton."

Dalton Meets the King, and Other Honors

In 1817, Dalton was elected president of his beloved Lit & Phil. The previous president, Thomas Henry, had died, and many thought that his son William would take over. He and Dalton were both vice presidents at the time. William insisted that Dalton take the presidency. Dalton agreed to serve in the office for a year, at which time William would take over. However, William's health was not good, so Dalton continued as president until his own death, twenty-seven years later.

A different kind of opportunity arose in 1818. Sir Humphry Davy asked Dalton to go along on Sir John Ross's Polar expeditions as scientific adviser. Although in good physical shape, Dalton was fifty-two years old and busy with students and experiments. He refused the chance.

For a time in the 1820s, Dalton became a teacher at a school again. He was the chemistry teacher at the Pine Street School of Medicine and Surgery in Manchester. For two years, Dalton taught "the first principles of chemistry, then applied them to investigations of material medica and other purposes relating to the medical profession," as described by a writer of a magazine article of the time. In 1822, he made his only trip across the English Channel and visited Paris. He intended, he wrote, "to spend a week or two in it and the environs; to visit a few of the chemical people who might be at home etc.:—to see the curiosities etc. etc."

He was able to meet many French scientists and mathematicians, including Arago, Fourier, Gay-Lussac, Humboldt, and Laplace. At Laplace's country home, one of Dalton's companions described: "As yet we had seen no one, when part of the company came in view at a distance; a gentleman of advanced years, and two young men. . . . We approached this group, when the elderly gentleman took off his hat, and advanced to give his hand to Dalton. It was Berthollet!"

As more scientists acknowledged the Atomic Theory, Dalton became more famous. Science, in general, was flourishing. In 1825, Michael Faraday discovered electromagnetic induction, the basis for our electrical industry. William Sturgeon made an electromagnet, and

Michael Faraday

George Stephenson built a steam locomotive that transformed railroads. The same year, King George IV decided to initiate awards of two gold medals to be given annually. The Royal Society met to determine the guidelines for the award of the medals, which would be given "for the most important discoveries or series of investigations completed and made known to the Royal Society in the year preceding the day of the award."

Men were honored with the awards, but the medals were not made until George IV's brother, William IV, became king in 1830. Then medals were given to the previous winners.

The first two recipients of the medals were John Dalton, for his discovery of the Atomic Theory, and James Ivory, for some mathematical work. The choice brought criticism because the guidelines had not been followed. Dalton had performed his Atomic Theory work almost twenty years before. Sir Humphry Davy, president of the Royal Society, discounted Dalton's contribution to understanding of the atom, stressing instead the theory proposed by Wollaston. However, he did praise Dalton's Theory of Definite Proportions, saying, his "permanent reputation will rest upon his having discovered a simple principle, the law of chemical combination."

When he was awarded the medal, Dalton traveled to London and met with the Royal Society for the first time. He had been a member for four years but had not attended the meetings.

Dalton hoped that Davy would come into his way of thinking about the Atomic Theory, but he never did. The charismatic Davy and the countrified Dalton had little in common, other than their love of science. In his final days, Davy wrote character sketches of men he had known. Of Dalton, he wrote, "John Dalton was a very singular man. A Quaker by profession and practice; he had none of the manners or ways of the world." He went on to imply that Dalton based his Atomic Theory on the ideas of others, including Davy, and called him "a coarse experimenter." Davy died in 1829 after a considerable scientific career, especially in the field of electricity and the discovery of elements.

Davy had been a foreign associate in the prestigious *Académie des sciences*. Only eight foreign associates at a time could belong to this French academy. Davy's death left an opening, and Dalton was chosen as a foreign associate member of what was one of the premier science associations of the time.

Even though Davy had little admiration for Dalton, others were impressed by him, including Charles Babbage. Babbage is known as the inventor of the Difference Engine, forerunner of today's computers. He also was a severe critic of the Royal Society, accusing the elite group of not understanding the technological advances of the Industrial

Revolution and allowing the world of science in Britain to lag behind that of other countries. Because of the deadwood that he saw in the Royal Society, he proposed a new, more vibrant organization. With the help of Dalton and others, the British Association for the Advancement of Science (BAAS) was born.

The first meeting of the BAAS was held in September 1831 in York. At the annual meetings, held in various places, scientific papers were presented, lectures and demonstrations were provided, and discussions took place day and night. Dalton was "seen for the first time by many who had long esteemed him at a distance." He was called Atomic Dalton.

Some of the younger chemists at the meeting campaigned for Dalton's Atomic Theory. They realized that a standard was needed for atomic weights. It was no good to have some using hydrogen equals one as a standard and others using other elements. Members of a Chemistry Committee declared, "Chemists should be enabled, by the most accurate experiments, to agree on the *relative weights of the several elements, Hydrogen, Oxygen, and Azote* [nitrogen], or what amounts to the same thing, that the specific gravity of the three gases should be ascertained in such a way as would insure the reasonable assent of all competent and unprejudiced judges." These young scientists not only accepted Dalton's theory, they were prepared to put it into action.

The second meeting of the BAAS was set for Oxford, site of one of the exclusive universities that Dalton could not attend or teach at because of his religion. However, Oxford had a special honor in mind for him. Through the efforts of friends and fellow scientists, Dalton was made an honorary Doctor of Civil Law. Physicist Michael Faraday, botanist Robert Brown, and scientist/inventor David Brewster also received the degree. Dalton had to wear the *scarlet* doctoral robes of Oxford, but with his color-blindness they did not appear to be red and go against his Quaker guidelines.

Since 1829, Babbage had been campaigning for Dalton to be awarded a civil pension. The government bestowed generous amounts to military men, clergy, relatives of politicians, and others, so Babbage figured that one of the leading men of science deserved the same. Others joined in, writing letters to members of Parliament and other government officials.

Charles Babbage

Finally, in 1833, Dalton was granted a pension of 150 pounds a year. The announcement was made at the third meeting of the BAAS, at the site of one of the other premier universities of the land, Cambridge. Adam Sedgewick, president of the association, made a flowery speech that ended with: "his Majesty, King William the Fourth, wishing to manifest his attachment to science, and his regard for a character like that of Dalton, had graciously conferred on him, out of the funds of the civil list, a substantial mark of his royal favor."

After the Johns family moved from Manchester, Dalton stayed in the house. His housekeeper, Susanna Ecroyd, cared for him. He still took the Johns sisters on his summer vacations, and they always remembered his kindness to them and their family.

Early in 1834, the city of Manchester and the Lit & Phil decided that their most famous citizen needed a monument. They began a subscription drive to raise money for one of three projects for John Dalton: a bust, a house with a laboratory, or a statue. A local newspaper stated, in overblown style: "We have the satisfaction of announcing that the scientific attainments of this distinguished philosopher are about to receive some suitable and public acknowledgement from his fellow townsmen. They are anxious to wipe away the reproach they have incurred by their unaccountable neglect of an individual who has raised the intellectual character of Manchester higher than that of Birmingham, or any other large mart of industry in the Kingdom."

A committee decided that a statue of Dalton would be appropriate, so they contacted a foremost sculptor, Francis Chantrey. He replied, "My price for a statue the size of life, whether sitting or standing, is two thousand guineas, including a suitable marble pedestal." He would need Dalton to come to London to pose for the sculpture.

By May 1834, Dalton was in London, staying at the house of G. W. Wood, member of Parliament from the Manchester area. Dalton was intrigued by the sculpting process and wrote to Peter Clare about it: "He took a profile as large as life by a camera lucida and then sketched a front view of the face on paper . . . told me I should see my head moulded in clay [the next morning] . . . the head having been formed from his drawings by some of his assistants. . . . On looking right and left, he found my ears were not alike, and the modeler had made them alike, so that he immediately cut off the left ear of the bust and made a new one more resembling the original."

While in London, Dalton visited and was praised by many famous people, including the Duke of Sussex, who was the president of the Royal Society at the time. To top it off, Babbage arranged an audience with King William IV.

King William IV

After the time for the audience was set, problems arose. Babbage wrote in a letter to Dalton's friend, William Charles Henry, about a conversation with Mr. Wood, the member of Parliament in whose house Dalton was staying: "Doctor Dalton, as a Quaker, could not appear in a court dress, because he must wear a sword. To this I replied, that being aware of the difficulty, I had proposed to let him wear the robes of a Doctor of Laws of Oxford. Mr. Wood remarked, that these robes being scarlet, they were not of a colour admissible by Quakers. To this I replied, that Doctor Dalton had a kind of colour-blindness, and that all red colours appeared to him to be the colour of dirt."

So it was planned that Dalton would wear his scarlet robes to see the king. To make sure Dalton was thoroughly trained in court etiquette, Babbage held several rehearsals. Chairs were placed to portray the Presence-chamber, and Babbage displayed the proper manners so Dalton could see the routine. Then the two of them went up to see the Difference Engine.

On the day of the audience, Babbage went to the house where Dalton was staying, and they rehearsed again—this time with the family taking part. Babbage was pleased with his "excellent friend, who followed his instructions as perfectly as if he had been repeating an experiment."

When they arrived at the court at St. James, attention was stirred because of Dalton's attire, but Babbage explained who he was. When they came before the king, Babbage wrote, "Doctor Dalton having kissed hands, the King asked him several questions, all of which the philosopher duly answered, and then moved on in proper order to join me." Still others noticed the fellow in Oxford robes. Babbage heard one person say, "Who the d___l is that fellow whom the King keeps talking to so long?"

All that we have recorded of Dalton's encounter with the king is in his account book: one guinea for the loan of a doctor's gown. Dalton is said to have told an old friend that the king asked, "Dr. Dalton, how are you getting on at Manchester?" He answered, "Well, I don't know; just middlin', I think." When his friend teased him about his lack of

A Doctor of Divinity.

Pub by Tabart & Cº June 4 1805 New Bond St.

A Doctor of Divinity, in a wig and an ordinary gown of black crape with a crimson hood behind—signifying a doctor of divinity at Oxford or Cambridge

court etiquette, Dalton replied in his Cumberland accent, "Mebby sae, but what can yan say to see like fowk?" ["Maybe so, but what can one say to folk like that?"]

Soon after the trip to London, Dalton took his usual summer holiday in Cumberland. He and the Johns sisters visited his old friend, William Alderson, who had studied with him and Elihu Robinson. Alderson told Miss Johns, "Ah, you see, ladies . . . he is not only a great but a good man, to think of such a humble person as I—he who has just been introduced to the King."

In September 1834, Dalton returned to Edinburgh for the annual meeting of the British Association for the Advancement of Science. While there, he was honored with a membership to the Royal Society of Edinburgh. The Town Council gave him the "freedom of the city," and the University of Edinburgh awarded him a doctorate degree.

In that same year, Dalton became a member of scientific societies of Berlin, Munich, and Moscow. He had truly become an international scientist.

He also remained a teacher, continuing his private tutoring business. He taught the young man who would become his most famous student. Benjamin Joule, a Manchester brewer, requested that Dalton teach chemistry to his two sons. Dalton requested that the two be already well studied in mathematics. Their former tutor said they were ready, but as J. P. Joule's biographer wrote later, "at the end of an hour, they had not got through addition. They attended, with some short breaks, twice a week for one hour, and at the end of two years had just got through arithmetic and the first book of Euclid when Dalton suggested that they should proceed to do the higher mathematics."

J. P. Joule later claimed that Dalton's lessons had fired his imagination and desire to learn more about science. He went on to become one of the founders of the theory of thermodynamics, and his name is immortalized as a unit of energy, the joule.

Dalton's brother, Jonathan, died of a stroke in December 1834. Because Jonathan had no heirs, he left John his entire estate. The house in which Dalton had been living was going to be torn down, so he used his inheritance to buy his own house. He was sixty-eight years old. Dalton also felt comfortable enough to replace his horn spoons with a set of silver spoons.

Legacy

In 1835, Dalton traveled to Dublin, Ireland, for the meeting of the British Association for the Advancement of Science. It was his last long trip, as he was beginning to feel his age. His last public appearance before a large audience seems to have been a lecture before the Manchester Mechanics Institution. On October 25, 1835, he spoke about the Atomic Theory to a full audience. The *Manchester Times* reported that "the lecture room was crowded in every part and the greatest anxiety was manifested by the audience not to lose a single word which fell from the lips of the speaker." A few months later, the institution presented Dalton with a silver inkstand, inscribed with his name, "in grateful acknowledgement of services rendered by their distinguished Townsman."

In June 1836, Dalton's civil pension was doubled to honor his accomplishments. Also that year, the BAAS met in Bristol. Dalton was able to go, and as a special treat he met again with Hannah Jepson, one of his early loves. In a letter to a cousin, he wrote: "We had a pleasant and interesting meeting at Bristol: my friend Peter Clare and I were most kindly entertained by Hannah Fisher (formerly H. Jepson of Lancaster) and her two daughters . . . and I had the additional pleasure of renewing an acquaintance of 40 Years standing."

Dalton had been healthy throughout his life. His doctors, Joseph Atkinson Ransome Sr. and Jr., attended him when needed. The younger doctor recalled the story of when his father treated Dalton for influenza. He gave him a dose of James' Powder to be taken at bedtime. When he saw Dalton the next day, he was better, so the doctor said the medicine must have worked. Dalton answered, "I do not well see how that can be, as I kept the powder until I could have an opportunity of analyzing it."

One spring evening in 1837, Dalton and a friend had an enthusiastic discussion about chemical symbols. Dalton was adamant about the superiority of his over those of Berzelius, and he stated his case vigorously. The next morning, on April 18, Dr. Ransome, Jr., was called to his home. He found Dalton "pale, speechless, and paralyzed on the right side; he appeared to recognize me by attempting to speak and move his left hand towards me." Dalton had suffered a stroke.

He recovered to some extent over the next few months. The Manchester Council allowed him to walk in the Botanical Gardens to recover his strength during his convalescence. After the stroke, he spoke slowly and carefully with some slurring of speech, but he was able to continue most of his daily activities.

In February 1838, he suffered a smaller stroke and recovered rapidly. His friend Peter Clare was often with him during these times, helping him walk and attending to other duties. Clare was a skilled clockmaker and as interested in science as Dalton was. People often saw the aged Dalton leaning on the arm of his friend as they crossed the street to the Lit & Phil.

After many delays, the Chantrey statue of Dalton was delivered to the Royal Manchester Institution. The work had taken twice as long as promised, but the town of Manchester was proud to receive it. Eventually, Dalton's statue stood in the entrance of the Manchester Town

John Dalton statue outside of Manchester's Town Hall

Hall across from his most famous student, J. P. Joule.

Dalton realized that his mental faculties were weaker. He complained to friends about his slowness in thinking and in experimenting.

In 1842, the BAAS met in Manchester. By custom as the leading scientist of the city, Dalton was designated president of the meeting, but he was too ill to handle the duties. In April 1844, he read his last paper for the Lit & Phil, entitled "On the fall of rain, etc., etc., in Manchester during a period of 50 years."

The Manchester Society accorded him one more

J. P. Joule, one of the founders of the theory of thermo dynamics, claimed that Dalton's lessons had fired his imagination and desire to learn more about science.

honor. On July 19, 1844, at their annual meeting, they passed a resolution stating "their admiration of the zeal and perseverance with which he has deduced the mean pressure and temperature of the atmosphere, and the quantity of rain for each month, and for the whole year; with the prevailing direction and force of the wind at different seasons in this neighbourhood, from a series of more than 200,000 observations, from the end of the year 1793 to the beginning of 1844, being a period of half a century." Dalton had written a reply that was read by Peter Clare: "I feel gratified by this testimony of kind regard offered to me by my old associates of the Literary and Philosophical Society of Manchester. At my age and under my infirmities, I can only thank you for this manifestation of sentiments, which I heartily reciprocate."

Eight days later, on July 27, Dalton died. On the 26th, his servant noticed that his hand was trembling when he wrote his daily weather observation: "a little rain this." Realizing he had left out a word, he added "day." He spent a restless night, and early in the morning the servant had to leave him and implored him not to move. Soon after, the housekeeper found Dalton mostly out of bed, his head on the floor. He had suffered another stroke. Dr. Ransome was called, but as he told Dalton's biographer, "I was again hastily summoned, but only to behold the lifeless body of my venerable friend."

Just as Dalton had requested, his eyes were removed to examine if any cause of his color deficiency could be found. Two doctors performed an autopsy and studied Dalton's eyes: "The aqueous was collected in a watch-glass from a careful puncture of the cornea, and viewed both by reflected and transmitted light, was found . . . free from colour. The vitreous humor and its envelope were also perfectly colorless." Dalton's theory for his color-blindness was false, but his last experiment had been performed.

The city of Manchester planned a glorious funeral for John Dalton. Lyon Playfair wrote, "When John Dalton died, on the 27th July, 1844, Manchester gave him the honours of a king. His body lay in state, and his funeral was like that of a monarch." As the city planned a public, spectacular funeral, the Society of Friends protested. As a simple Quaker, Dalton probably would have been appalled at the pomp. However, the people's desire to show their appreciation to the great scientist of their city overruled the Quaker sentiments.

Dalton's coffin lay in state in the Town Hall. On August 10, 1844, the hall was opened to the public, and more than 40,000 people paid their respects. On Monday, August 12, the coffin was escorted to Ardwick Cemetery. The procession was almost a mile long. The hearse was followed by a hundred carriages carrying leading citizens, and many more citizens followed on foot. The route was lined with hundreds more. In a book about the history of Manchester, the author wrote,

"Most of the mills and workshops were closed, as were also the whole of the shops in the principal streets of the town."

After the public funeral, Dalton's body was buried by his fellow Quakers. Later, a granite slab was placed on the grave, inscribed with "JOHN DALTON" and the dates of his birth and death. When the Ardwick Cemetery was sold, the slab was transferred to the Lit & Phil. Elizabeth Patterson wrote in her 1970 biography of Dalton, "The graveyard has become the site of a children's playground, put to a daily use that its plain, kindly Quaker inhabitant would surely approve."

In his will, Dalton left funds for family and friends and an endowment for a professorship of chemistry at Oxford. However, another clause revoked this endowment to help the Johns family in a time of financial loss for them. Dalton bequeathed his scientific equipment to William Charles Henry and his manuscripts and correspondence to Henry and three executors. Henry was in continental Europe at the time of his friend's death, and so the papers were collected by Clare. Eventually, Henry was able to obtain them, and he wrote the first biography of Dalton.

When a famous painter, Ford Madox Brown, was commissioned to decorate the Great Hall of Town Hall, one of his pictures showed Dalton collecting marsh gas (methane) for his experiments. In 1903, the city celebrated the centennial of Dalton's Atomic Theory, and in 1966 they paid tribute to him on the bicentennial of his birth.

Dalton showed that a person didn't have to attend the most prestigious college or have the best family connections to make contributions in the field of science. His curiosity and perseverance led to some of the greatest scientific ideas of the 1800s.

His legacy can be seen in modern chemistry textbooks, where his Atomic Theory is listed and explained, even though much of it has been proven wrong.

A replication of an atom

In 1897, Joseph John Thomson, professor of physics and director of the Cavendish Laboratory at Cambridge University, announced the discovery of electrons. Dalton's solid, ball-like atom was not the ultimate particle, but a mass made up of particles. Thomson found that electrons are identical regardless of the type of atom to which they belong. He also discovered that they carry a negative charge. Thomson proposed a "plum pudding atom," with electrons stuck in a mass of positive charge producing neutral charged atoms. His discovery met with great skepticism, but in the early 1900s other scientists discovered that the atom was divisible.

The discoveries of X-rays and radioactivity brought even more disintegration to the solid atom. In studying radioactivity, Ernest Rutherford found a tiny hard mass in the center of atoms. He called the particles protons, from a Greek word for "first importance." In 1932, Sir James Chadwick discovered a neutrally charged particle in the nucleus of atoms, which he called the neutron. Three particles had been found in what Dalton had assumed was the indivisible atom.

After the 1930s, scientists discovered even more tiny particles hidden in atoms. Particles with exotic names, such as neutrino and gluon, have been found, and more may be announced in the future.

Dmitri Mendeleev

Moreover, the phenomenon of radioactivity showed that atoms are not unchangeable. When radioactive atoms decay, they change to another element.

Dalton's legacy also includes the development of the Periodic Table by Dmitri Mendeleev and the knowledge that allowed organic chemists to synthesize a multitude of new molecules, from medicines to synthetic rubbers and dyes to plastics.

The dalton is an alternate name for the unified atomic mass unit (u or amu). The dalton is often used in microbiology and biochemistry to state the masses of large organic molecules; these measurements are typically in kilodaltons (kDa). It seems necessary to have such a unit, since "kilo-amu" would be such a clumsy name. The SI (International System of Units) accepts the dalton as an alternate name for the unified atomic mass unit and specifies Da as its proper symbol.

Since 1997, the European Geological Society has awarded the John Dalton Medal for outstanding work in hydrology.

Frank Greenaway, a biographer of Dalton, summed up his contribution this way: "the idea that the material world at our fingertips is made of atoms which we have the power to re-arrange in new ways is the master-concept of our age. . . . This was the deed of John Dalton and surely entitles him to honour and gratitude."

John Dalton

Timeline

1766	Born in Eaglesfield, England.
1778	Teaches school in Eaglesfield.
1781	Begins teaching school in Kendal.
1785	Buys a school with his brother, Jonathan.
1787	Begins a meteorological observation notebook.
1791	Completes a botanical sample book.
1793	Hired as a professor at New College in Manchester; publishes *Meteorological Essays and Observations*.
1794	Becomes a member of the Manchester Literary and Philosophical Society; writes a paper on color–blindness.
1796	Attends lectures by Dr. Thomas Garnett, which may spark his interest in chemistry.
1800	Elected secretary of the Manchester Literary and Philosophical Society.
1801	Writes essays on mixed gases and water vapor.
1803	Prepares the first tables of atomic weights.
1804	Discusses the Atomic Theory with Thomas Thomson.
1807	Discusses the Atomic Theory in Scotland.
1808	Publishes *A New System of Chemical Philosophy*, Volume 1: Part 1; becomes vice president of the Manchester Literary and Philosophical Society.
1810	Publishes *A New System of Chemical Philosophy*, Volume 1: Part 2.
1817	Elected president of the Manchester Literary and Philosophical Society.
1822	Becomes a fellow of the Royal Society.
1826	Granted the Royal Medal.
1827	Publishes *A New System of Chemical Philosophy*, Volume 2: Part 1.
1830	Elected into the French *Académie des sciences*.
1831	Becomes a founding member of the British Association for the Advancement of Science.
1832	Receives an honorary degree from Oxford University.
1834	Accepts an honorary degree from Edinburgh University.
1837	Suffers his first stroke.
1844	Dies on July 27.

Sources

CHAPTER ONE: *A Quaker Boy*
p. 9,   "Yes. Will you sit . . ." Frank Greenaway, *John Dalton and the Atom* (Ithaca, NY: Cornell University Press, 1966), 186.
p. 13,   "the greatest schools of . . ." Elizabeth C. Patterson, *John Dalton and the Atomic Theory* (Garden City, NY: Doubleday & Company, 1970), 14.
p. 13,   "Yan med due't . . ." Henry Enfield Roscoe, *John Dalton and the Rise of Modern Chemistry* (New York: MacMillan and Company, 1895), 19.
p. 14,   "for both sexes at reasonable . . ." Greenaway, *John Dalton and the Atom*, 60.

CHAPTER TWO: *Young Teacher*
p. 18,   "Jonathan & John Dalton respectfully . . ." Robert Angus Smith, *Memoir of John Dalton and History of the Atomic Theory up to His Time* (London: Manchester Literary and Philosophical Society, 1856), 12.
p. 18,   "Twelve lectures of Natural Philosophy . . ." Ibid., 14.
p. 19,   "Methinks I see him now . . ." Smith, *Memoir of John Dalton and History of the Atomic Theory up to His Time*, 11.
p. 19,   "He is, perhaps, one of . . ." Patterson, *John Dalton and the Atomic Theory*, 28.
p. 19,   "Mr. Gough was as much gratified . . ." Roscoe, *John Dalton and the Rise of Modern Chemistry*, 33.
p. 20,   "In the evening, soon after . . ." Patterson, *John Dalton and the Atomic Theory*, 31.
p. 21,   "[I] dried and pressed a . . ." Ibid., 32.
p. 21,   "nothing that enjoys animal life . . ." Ibid., 33.
p. 24,   "The occasion of my addressing . . ." Ibid., 34.
p. 24,   "Evacuation S[olid?] L[iquid?] . . ." Greenaway, *John Dalton and the Atom*, 66.
p. 24,   "As I have thought thy talents . . ." Patterson, *John Dalton and the Atomic Theory*, 36.
p. 24,   "I think they are both . . ." Ibid., 37.
p. 24,   "I cannot say that I have . . ." Greenaway, *John Dalton and the Atom*, 67.
pp. 25–26,   "I may answer that my . . ." Roscoe, *John Dalton and the Rise of Modern Chemistry*, 122.
p. 26,   "a dried specimen of the lady's slipper . . ." Ibid.

CHAPTER THREE: *Meteorological Observations and Essays*
pp. 27–28,   "As the number of these . . ." Greenaway, *John Dalton and the Atom*, 71.
p. 28,   "supposed 40 to 50 miles . . ." John Dalton, *Meteorological Observations and Essays*, second edition (London: Harris and Crossfield, 1834), 2.
p. 28,   "[the] discovery promised . . ." Ibid., 5.

p. 29,   "Philosophers [scientists] are generally persuaded . . ." Ibid., 17.
p. 29,   "an internal vibratory motion . . ." Ibid.
p. 30,   "an instrument meant to show . . ." Ibid., 30.
p. 30,   "the greater the number of the scale . . ." Ibid., 31.
p. 30,   "it is very inadequate . . ." Ibid., 32.
p. 31,   "Sometimes the appearance is that . . ." Ibid., 53.
p. 31,   "The height of the arch . . ." Ibid., 231.
p. 34,   "the beams were guided . . ." Ibid., 148.
p. 34,   "The light of the aurora has . . ." Ibid., 168.
p. 36,   "Upon consideration of the facts . . ." Ibid., 127.
p. 36,   "condensed into water by cold . . ." Ibid., 132.
p. 37,   "Since the barometer has become . . ." Ibid., 138.
pp. 37–38, "a thought occurred to me . . ." Ibid., 203.

CHAPTER FOUR: *I'm Color-blind?*
p. 39,   "other learned professions . . ." Patterson, *John Dalton and the Atomic Theory*, 46.
p. 39,   "a gentleman to fill the situation . . ." Ibid., 44.
p. 40,   "Our academy is a large . . ." Ibid., 53.
p. 40,   "There is in this town a large library . . ." Ibid., 54.
p. 42,   "Thou hast bought me . . ." Roscoe, *John Dalton and the Rise of Modern Chemistry*, 70.
p. 42,   "Since the year 1790 . . ." Greenaway, *John Dalton and the Atom*, 99.
p. 43,   "Notwithstanding this, I was never convinced . . ." Ibid.
p. 43,   "This observation clearly proved . . ." Ibid., 100.
pp. 43–45, "distinguish six kinds of colour . . ." Patterson, *John Dalton and the Atomic Theory*, 62.
p. 45,   "Woollen yarn dyed crimson . . ." Roscoe, *John Dalton and the Rise of Modern Chemistry*, 78.
p. 45,   "Hence it will be immediately . . ." Ibid., 79.
pp. 45–46, "the difference between day–light . . ." Patterson, *John Dalton and the Atomic Theory*, 62.
p. 46,   "I must admit that Mr. . . ." Roscoe, *John Dalton and the Rise of Modern Chemistry*, 87.
p. 48,   "I think they [other grammar books] are . . ." Ibid., 76.
p. 48,   "Grammatically speaking, therefore . . ." Smith, *Memoir of John Dalton and History of the Atomic Theory up to His Time*, 35.

CHAPTER FIVE: *Fascination with Gases*
p. 50,   "an elastic fluid *sui generis* . . ." Greenaway, *John Dalton and the Atom*, 108.
p. 54,   "in a cold morning . . ." Ibid., 112.
p. 56,   "The density of elastic fluids . . ." Ibid., 115.
p. 56,   "When two elastic fluids [gases] . . ." Ibid., 114.
p. 56,   "can scarcely be a doubt . . ." Patterson, *John Dalton and the Atomic Theory*, 90.
p. 57,   "The object of the present Essay . . ." Greenaway, *John Dalton and the Atom*, 119.

p. 57,   "when the temperature of . . ." Ibid.

p. 57,   "All elastic fluids expand the same . . ." Patterson, *John Dalton and the Atomic Theory*, 92.

pp. 57–58, "In the discussions . . ." Ibid., 94.

CHAPTER SIX: *The Atomic Theory Is Born*

p. 60,   "It seems probable to me . . ." Patterson, *John Dalton and the Atomic Theory*, 107.

p. 61,   "we apply the term *elements* . . ." William H. Brock, *The Norton History of Chemistry* (New York: W. W. Norton & Company, 1992), 129.

p. 61,   "I have been, as usual . . ." Patterson, *John Dalton and the Atomic Theory*, 123.

p. 61,   "Why does water not admit . . ." Ibid., 124.

pp. 64–65, "My attention has been directed . . ." Ibid., 142.

p. 65,   "To the Professors of the Universities . . ." Ibid., 144.

p. 65,   "This power of conducting heat . . ." John Dalton, *A New System of Chemical Philosophy* (New York: Philosophical Library, 1964), 79.

p. 65,   "the specific gravity of ice . . ." Ibid., 104.

p. 66,   "Chemical analysis and synthesis . . ." Ibid., 162.

p. 66,   "Now it is one great object . . ." Ibid., 163.

p. 67,   "If there are two bodies . . ." Ibid.

p. 67,   "The following general rules may . . ." Ibid., 167.

CHAPTER SEVEN: *Controversy and New Symbols*

p. 71,   "In the autumn of 1807 . . ." Thomas Thomson, *The History of Chemistry* (London: Henry Colburn and Richard Bentley, 1830), 293.

p. 72,   "that when our views are . . ." Greenaway, *John Dalton and the Atom*, 156.

p. 73,   "These ratios by volume are . . ." Patterson, *John Dalton and the Atomic Theory*, 176.

p. 74,   "his [Gay–Lussac's] notion of measures . . ." Ibid., 179.

p. 75,   "such a doctrine of the composition . . ." Ibid., 183.

p. 75,   "Never has a present given . . ." Ibid., 185.

p. 76,   "When three or more particles . . ." Ibid., 188.

p. 76,   "the new signs . . . are destined . . ." Ibid.

pp. 76–77, "Berzelius' symbols are horrifying . . ." William Charles Henry, *Memoirs of the Life and Scientific Researches of John Dalton* (London: Harrison and Sons, 1854), 124.

p. 77,   "I do not, however, approve . . ." Ibid.

pp. 77–78, "As my mother was standing . . ." Patterson, *John Dalton and the Atomic Theory*, 157.

p. 78,   "I may mention that my sister . . ." Ibid., 236.

p. 80,   "My friend, Mr. Ewart . . ." Henry, *Memoirs of the Life and Scientific Researches of John Dalton*, 124.

p. 80,   "Atoms are round bits . . ." Brock, *The Norton History of Chemistry*, 128.

CHAPTER EIGHT: *Dalton Meets the King, and Other Honors*

pp. 81–82, "the first principles of chemistry . . ." Patterson, *John Dalton and the Atomic Theory*, 214.

p. 82, "As yet we had seen no . . ." Ibid., 210.

p. 82, "for the most important discoveries . . ." Ibid., 217.

p. 83, "permanent reputation will rest . . ." Ibid., 219.

p. 83, "John Dalton was a very singular . . ." Ibid., 220.

p. 84, "seen for the first time . . ." Ibid., 225.

p. 84, "Chemists should be enabled . . ." Ibid., 230.

p. 85, "his Majesty, King William the Fourth . . ." Ibid., 234.

pp. 85–86, "We have the satisfaction of announcing . . ." Ibid., 237.

p. 86, "My price for a statue . . ." Ibid., 238.

p. 86, "He took a profile as large . . ." Ibid., 239.

p. 87, "Doctor Dalton, as a Quaker, . . ." Ibid., 242.

p. 87, "excellent friend, who followed . . ." Ibid., 243.

p. 87, "Doctor Dalton having kissed hands . . ." Ibid., 245.

p. 87, "Who the d___l is that . . ." Ibid.

p. 87, "Well, I don't know; just middlin' . . ." Ibid., 247.

p. 89, "Mebby sae, but what can . . ." Ibid.

p. 89, "Ah, you see, ladies . . ." Ibid.

p. 89, "at the end of an hour . . ." Ibid., 252.

CHAPTER NINE: *Legacy*

p. 91, "the lecture room was crowded . . ." Patterson, *John Dalton and the Atomic Theory*, 257.

p. 91, "in grateful acknowledgement of services . . ." Ibid.

pp. 91–92, "We had a pleasant and interesting . . ." Ibid., 258.

p. 92, "I do not well see how . . ." Henry, *Memoirs of the Life and Scientific Researches of John Dalton*, 218.

p. 92, "pale, speechless, and paralyzed . . ." Patterson, *John Dalton and the Atomic Theory*, 259.

p. 94, "their admiration of the zeal . . ." Greenaway, *John Dalton and the Atom*, 198.

pp. 94–95, "I feel gratified by this . . ." Ibid.

p. 95, "I was again hastily summoned . . ." Henry, *Memoirs of the Life and Scientific Researches of John Dalton*, 201.

p. 95, "The aqueous was collected . . ." Ibid.

p. 95, "When John Dalton died, on . . ." Patterson, *John Dalton and the Atomic Theory*, 277.

p. 96, "Most of the mills and workshops . . ." Ibid., 278.

p. 96, "The graveyard has become . . ." Ibid., 279.

p. 99, "the idea that the material . . ." Greenaway, *John Dalton and the Atom*, 227.

Bibliography

Brock, William. *The Norton History of Chemistry*. New York: W. W. Norton & Company, 1992.

Cardwell, D. S. L., ed. *John Dalton and the Progress of Science*. Manchester, England: Manchester University Press, 1968.

Dalton, John. *Meteorological Observations and Essays*. London: Harris and Crossfield, 1834.

———. *A New System of Chemical Philosophy*. New York: Philosophical Library, 1964.

Greenaway, Frank. *John Dalton and the Atom*. Ithaca, NY: Cornell University Press, 1966.

Patterson, Elizabeth C. *John Dalton and the Atomic Theory*. Garden City, NY: Doubleday & Company, 1970.

Roscoe, Henry Enfield. *John Dalton and the Rise of Modern Chemistry*. New York: MacMillan and Company, 1895.

Salzberg, Hugh W. *From Caveman to Chemist: Circumstances and Achievements*. Washington: American Chemical Society, 1991.

Smith, Robert Angus. *Memoir of John Dalton and History of the Atomic Theory up to His Time*. London: Manchester Literary and Philosophical Society, 1856.

Whiting, Jim, and Marylou Morano Kjelle. *John Dalton and the Atomic Theory*. Hockessin, Delaware: Mitchell Lane Publishers, 2005.

Web sites

http://antoine.frostburg.edu/chem/senese/101/atoms/dalton.shtml

An excellent site on which you can explore Dalton's Atomic Theory. Created by Fred Senese in the Department of Chemistry at Frostburg State University, in Maryland, the site includes a short biography, key vocabulary words associated with Atomic Theory, and a breakdown of Dalton's assumptions. You can even take an interactive quiz on Dalton's theory to test your knowledge.

http://webserver.lemoyne.edu/faculty/giunta/dalton.html

On this site are excerpts from Dalton's *A New System of Chemical Philosophy*, published in 1808. It also includes Dalton's table of atomic weights and scanned atomic symbols.

http://rylibweb.man.ac.uk/dalton/exhib.html

"John Dalton: Manchester Man" is the title of an online exhibit at John Rylands University Library, University of Manchester, in England. The exhibit has information on Dalton's life, his Atomic Theory, and his legacy.

http://www.chemistrydaily.com/chemistry/John_Dalton

Chemistry Daily, a free resource for chemistry students, features a biography of Dalton on this site, which is hosted by The Chemistry Encyclopedia.

Index

Alderson, William, 14, 89
atoms, 59–61, *96–97*, 98
Aurora Borealis, 31, *32–33*, 34–35
Avogadro, Amedeo, 73–75

Babbage, Charles, 83–85, *85*, 87
Barnes, Thomas, 39
barometers, 20, 27–29, 35, 37
Berthollet, Claude, 73, 82
Berzelius, Johann Jakob, 75–76, *75*, 92
Bewley, George, 17–18, 24
Black, Joseph, 64
Boyle, Robert, 37, 53, 60, 70
Boyle's Law, 56
Brewster, David, 84
British Association for the Advancement of Science (BAAS), 84–85, 89, 91, 94
Brown, Ford Madox, 96
Brown, Robert, 84

Chadwick, James, 98
Chantrey, Francis, 86, 92
Charles' Law, 57
chemical symbols, 76–77
Chentham Library, 40, *40*
Clare, Peter, 18, 86, 92, 94, 96
Coleridge, Samuel Taylor, 16
color–blind test, *44–45*
Crosthwaite, Peter, 19, 21, 27, 29–31

Dalton, Abigail Fearon (grandmother), 10
Dalton, Deborah Greenup (mother), 10, 42
Dalton, John, *6, 8, 100*
   atomic theory, 61, 63, 66–68, 71–78, 80, 83, 84
   audience with King William IV, 86–87, 89
   and botany, 21, 23, 42
   character, 13, 16, 18, 77–78, 83
   and chemistry, 40–41, 54, 70, 81, 89, 96
   color–blindness, 41–43, 45–47, 84, 87, 95
   controversies, 52, 57–58, 71–73, 75–77
   death, 95–96
   education, 11, 13–14
   Elements of English Grammar, 47–48

eyes, donation to science, 47, 95
and gases, 53, 55–58, 61, 64, 73–75
health, 92, 94–95
honors and awards, 81–87, 89, 91, 94–95
interest in math, 15, 18
later years, 90–92, 94
as a lecturer, 63–65, 72, 91
legacy, 96, 98–99
and meteorology, 20, 26–29
Meterological Observations and Essays, 27–31, 34–38, 49
New System of Chemical Philosophy, 65, 74–75
as a professor, 24, 39
religious beliefs, 11, 72, 84, 87, 95
scientific writings, 16, 18, 21, 27, 50–51, 53–58, 61, 94
social life and relationships, 25–26, 40, 77–78, 85, 89, 91–92
statue of, 85–86, 92, *93*, 94
as a teacher, 14–18, 21, 24, 77, 81–82, 89
youth, 10–11, 42
Dalton, Jonathan (brother), 10, 17–18, 21, 25–26, 40, 43, 45, 90
Dalton, Jonathan (grandfather), 10
Dalton, Jonathan (uncle), 10
Dalton, Joseph (father), 10, 21
Dalton, Mary (sister), 10, 18
Daltonism, 46
Dalton's Atomic Theory, 9, 65–66, *69*, 70–71, 73, 75, 78, 82–84, 91, 96
Dalton's Law of Partial Pressures, 56
Davy, Sir Humphrey, 64, 71, 72, 81, 83
Dissenters, 11, 13, 39

evaporation, 35–36, 51, 57
Ewart, Peter, 80

Fahrenheit scale, 30
Faraday, Michael, 56, 82, *82*, 84
Fletcher, John, 13–14
Fox, George, 11
Franklin, Benjamin, 14, 41

Garnett, Thomas, 40
Gassendi, Pierre, 60
Gay–Lussac, Joseph, 73–74, *74*, 82
George IV, King, 82
Gough, John, 19–20, 24, 39, 57
Greenup, Thomas, 24

Hale, Stephen, 50
Henry, Thomas, 40–41, 81
Henry, William, 41, 57, 64
Henry, William Charles, 10, 41, 87, 96
Henry's Law, 58
hygrometers, 20, 27, 30

Industrial Revolution, 49, 83–84
Ivory, James, 83

Jepson, Hannah, 25–26, 91–92
John Dalton Medal, 99
Johns, William, 77–78, 85, 96
Joule, J. P., 89, *94*

Kinetic Theory of Gases, 53

Lavoisier, Antoine, 41, *41*, 61, 66
Law of Definite Proportions, 70, 72

Manchester, England, *25, 92*
Manchester Literary and Philosophical Society, 10, 26, 41, 50, 54, 81, 85, 94–95
Mendeleev, Dmitri, 98

New College, 24, 39, 45, 77
Newton, Isaac, *14–15*, 29, 53, 55, 60, *60*, 70

Periodic Table, 63, 98
Priestley, Joseph, 41

Quakers (Society of Friends), 10–11, *12*, 13, 72, 87, 95

Ransome, Joseph Atkinson, 92, 95
Reaumer's scale, 30
Richter, J. B., 75
Robinson, Elihu, 13–15, 19, 24, 48, 89
Roscoe, Henry, 10, 13, 26, 46
Royal Institution (London), 63, 72
Royal Manchester Institution, 92
Royal Society, 29, 46, 72, 78, 82–84, 89
Rutherford, Ernest, 98

Science Museum of London, *79*, 80
Sedgewick, Adam, 85
Smith, R. A., 10
Southey, Robert, 16
Stephenson, George, 82
Sturgeon, William, 82

table of relative weights, 61, *62–63*, 63–64, 66–68, 84
The Gentleman's Diary magazine, 15–16, 21
The Ladies' Diary magazine, 15–16, 21
theodolite, 31
Theory of Definite Proportions, 83
thermometers, 20, 27, 29–30
Thomas, William, 81
Thomson, Joseph John, 98
Thomson, Thomas, 64, 71

Volta, Alexander, 41

water cycle, 50–51, *51*
William IV, King, 82–83, 86–87, *86*
Wollaston, William Hyde, 71–72, 83
Wood, G. W., 86
Wordsworth, William, 16, 19

Young, Thomas, 47

Picture Credits

All images used in this book that are not in the public domain are credited in the listing that follows:

6:       Courtesy of the Library of Congress
8:       Robert Harding Picture Library Ltd / Alamy
12:     Classic Image / Alamy
14–15: North Wind Picture Archives / Alamy
20:     Courtesy of Ed Morgan
22–23: mauritius images GmbH / Alamy
25:     Rohan Van Twest / Alamy
28:     Used under license from iStockphoto.com
32–33: Used under license from iStockphoto.com
35:     Courtesy of Ed Morgan
36–37: Used under license from iStockphoto.com
40:     Courtesy of terry6082 Books
41:     Courtesy of Jastrow
43:     Courtesy of Spigget
44–45: Used under license from iStockphoto.com
51:     Used under license from iStockphoto.com
54–55: Used under license from iStockphoto.com
56:     Used under license from iStockphoto.com
65:     Used under license from iStockphoto.com
77:     Used under license from iStockphoto.com
79:     ImageState / Alamy
86:     The Print Collector / Alamy
88:     Florilegius / Alamy
93:     Courtesy of Kaihsu Tai
94:     Courtesy of Kaihsu Tai
96–97: Used under license from iStockphoto.com
98:     http://en.wikipedia.org/wiki/File:Medeleeff_by_repin.jpg
100:   bilwissedition Ltd. & Co. KG / Alamy